Advance Praise

"By sharing the darkness she traveled in her experience with an eating disorder, Ally Rae Pesta gives voice to the devastation this mental illness causes and the bravery required to reclaim one's self-worth."

—Jennifer Kreatsoulas, PhD
Founder of Yoga for Eating Disorders
and author of *The Courageous Path to Healing*

"Ally's story is one of human discovery that sits alongside the fierce determination to heal. This book is for everyone who has battled their inner demons—not just an eating disorder, but any kind of addiction."

—Tammy Lyons
Founder of Inner Bliss Yoga & Believe in Cle

"*Beyond My Body* is a captivating and intimate, behind-the-scenes view of the human experience of an eating disorder. Ally lends a powerful voice to the conversation around self-worth, mental wellness, and eating disorders."

—Jason Wood
author of *Starving for Survival*

"This breathtaking and glorious memoir weaves tragedy and triumph together in ways that remind us life is best lived outside the boundaries of our physical bodies and the path to self-love is best experienced in the mystery of always becoming someone new."

—**Stephanie Diaz**
Podcast host Runner's Round Table
and founder of Cor.rer Retreats

"Anyone working toward healing their relationship with their body would be lucky to read *Beyond My Body*. Ally's writing makes you feel like you've known her for forever, where you're impacted by reading her book all at once and later come back to read each vignette and have that same impact."

—**Rebecca Edmonds**
Anti-Diet Coach, @recoveryrebecca

"As a parent of teen daughters and an adolescent educator, Ally's memoir is a valuable resource and honest portrayal of the complex origins and mental health challenges of eating disorders for girls and young women. Through beautifully written vignettes, *Beyond My Body* offers a unique story of hope, healing, and empowerment, showing we are all truly 'enough.'"

—**Aimee Tapajna McNamee**
Educator, Artist, and Parent

"This book is about much more than recovering from an eating disorder. It's about breaking down, building up, being okay and then not so okay, crying, smiling, becoming, and being human. An absolute must read."

—**Cambria Camp**
Eating Disorder Recovery Coach

"Ally poignantly portrays the long arc of the eating disorder struggle from the traumas that instigate dissociating from her body to the many courageous, small, moments that lead to kindly reclaiming herself. This book is a heartbreakingly honest affirmation that eating disorder recovery is not easy but is possible."

—**Daneen Farrall**
EYRT 200; Eat Breathe Thrive™ Yoga
for Eating Disorder Recovery Facilitator

"Ally has a remarkable way of walking you through her journey in a vivid and beautiful way. Her work is an astonishing reminder of how strong and resilient the human mind and body can be, the importance of connectivity within and around you, and the vast capacity of healing."

—**Ally Barry**
Physical Therapist, DPT

"The authentic journey of *Beyond My Body* makes this required reading for all those struggling with any level of an eating disorder. You will learn about finding peace with food, embracing body acceptance, deconstructing limiting beliefs, and permitting yourself to move forward with compassion."

—**Brenda Lamparyk**
Integrative Health Coach, Personal Trainer,
Brain Health Advocate

"A brave narrative of human struggle, recovery, and what it means to face your harshest critic (yourself) and come out stronger than ever. You'll find yourself transported to a young girl's side in these pages, relating to her suffering in the pursuit of perfection, crying with her, laughing with her and celebrating her every painful step toward learning she is enough just by being herself."

—**Liz McKinney**
M.S. in Clinical Nutrition and
Certified Nutrition Specialist (CNS)

"In this deeply moving memoir, Ally Rae Pesta fearlessly shares her journey of living with, and ultimately overcoming, her eating disorder. This page-turner masterfully weaves together vulnerability and strength to tell a story of resilience, self-discovery, and self-acceptance, while also addressing the complexities of a harrowing mental health condition."

—Jocelyn Skoler
Licensed Master's Social Work (LMSW)

"The inner dialogue Ally shares in each of her stories is one that so many of us have spoken to ourselves but wouldn't dare share out loud. Her bold declaration of hurting and healing is one that I know will inspire women of all ages to know that they are not alone in reclaiming wholeness and body love."

—Lauren Seipel
Owner of Rising Rooted, empowering women through movement, health education, and community building

"Ally shares her story in a raw and honest way. She exposes many of the societal issues around weight, body image, diet culture, and sexual assault that so many young people face. *Beyond My Body* is an important read for girls and women of all ages, parents, and truly anyone who wishes to redefine their worth."

—Tucker Grose
Entrepreneur, endurance athlete, coach

"I learned so much about complex eating disorders and the mental exhaustion it takes to silently push through. This book is a wonderful testimony that you don't have to struggle alone, and that you CAN take back your power and worth!"

—Alysia McKean
Founder of The Mat Project, Bachelor of Science and Health Promotion, Certified Yoga Teacher

"Ally takes us on a vulnerable life journey with an active eating disorder and the perseverance to unlearn distorted thinking and behaviors. Her beautiful story is one of resilience and commitment to finding wholeness inside and out. *Beyond My Body* will help those diagnosed with an eating disorder and the many people who have a difficult relationship with food, exercise, and body image."

—Jennifer Borovica
Licensed Independent Social Worker,
owner Rebel Rising Wellness

"Ally Rae's book is a priceless gift to all young women struggling with an eating disorder. She shares her story with pure honesty. I recommend this book to any young girl who struggles with the dangers of trying to be accepted versus making accepting herself the first priority."

—Petra Robinson
CEO of Petra Robinson Inc
and Zumba Fitness industry adviser

Beyond My Body

Beyond My Body

Recovering from a Complex Eating Disorder, Reclaiming Movement, and Finding My Worth

ALLY RAE PESTA

Peacock Proud PRESS

Beyond My Body: Recovering from a Complex Eating Disorder, Reclaiming Movement, and Finding My Worth

First Published in the USA in 2023 by Peacock Proud Press, Phoenix, Arizona

ISBN 978-1-957232-13-3 Hardback
ISBN 978-1-957232-15-7 Paperback
ISBN 978-1-957232-16-4 eBook

Library of Congress Control Number: 2023915959

Editors
Laura L. Bush, PhD, peacockproud.com
Wendy Ledger, votype.com
Babette Dunkelgrun

Cover Design
Jana Linnell

Interior Layout
Medlar Publishing Solutions Pvt Ltd., India

Portrait Photographer
Ryland Lovvorn, rylocreative.com

DISCLAIMER:
This is a work of nonfiction. The information is of a general nature to help readers know and understand more about orthorexia and healing from eating disorders. Readers of this publication agree that Ally Rae Pesta and Peacock Proud Press will not be held responsible or liable for damages that may be alleged or resulting directly or indirectly from their use of this publication. All external links are provided as a resource only and are not guaranteed to remain active for any length of time. The author or publisher cannot be held accountable for the information provided by, or actions resulting from, accessing these resources.

To Mama, Daddy, and Sissy:
Thank you for never giving up. You all saved my life.

To my seventeen-year-old self:
Thank you for still loving me when I could not love you.

To every soul who reads this:
Know you are enough.

Content Warning

This memoir discusses eating disorders, sexual assault, and suicidal thoughts. Please take note and take care of yourself while reading. The information in this book is solely based on my personal experience and should not be used in place of any medical advice. If you or a loved one are suffering from a mental health condition, an eating disorder, and/or disordered eating, please consult with a medical professional.

The stories in this book are recreated from my personal memories of them. Some names and identifying information have been changed to protect the privacy of the individuals.

Recovery Resources

If you or a loved one need support for recovery, there is hope!

Visit

National Eating Disorders
(NEDA Feeding Hope)
https://www.nationaleatingdisorders.org/

Project Heal
https://www.theprojectheal.org/

ANAD
https://anad.org/

or
any **local recovery centers** in your area.

Mental Health Resources

If you or a loved one are experiencing mental health distress,
call or text the **988 Suicide Crisis Lifeline**
to reach a trained crisis counselor.

Chat at **988lifeline.org**.

Calls are free and confidential.

Table of Contents

PART 5

Prologue: Fitting through the Right Doors

"Don't eat that, or you won't fit through the door," my father says whenever I grab an extra handful of Cheetos or serve myself a hefty scoop of vanilla and chocolate chip cookie dough in the "I love ice cream" bowl. My father often makes this comment to me. In a house, a standard door measures thirty-six inches across or three feet wide.

How much ice cream could I eat before I fail to fit through a door? How many chocolate chips? How many Cheetos? As a young girl, I try to laugh it off. Yet that phrase constantly lingers in my mind, like elevator music, subtle but always there: "Don't eat that, or you won't fit through the door."

We aren't an overly health-conscious family. We aren't like the Hirshes, who eat green peppers for breakfast, whose parents never allow a single piece of junk food in their home. My dad eats a half pint of ice cream every night before bed. Yet his daily five-mile run "counters" his indulgence. He still fits through doors.

I must also be able to fit through doors, so I follow my dad's lead. I can eat curly fries at lunch, but I must burn off those calories at volleyball practice that night. The doors I long to pass through are only open if I'm fit enough to move through them. To win my dad's approval, I must go through special doors, ones that aren't standard size, ones that only small, fit humans can pass through. These doors lead to success and opportunity, as the world rewards those who are fit. My dad understands fitness is often a sign of determination, well-being, and drive. Normal-size doors are for average humans. But If I continue my fitness regimen, I will be able to go through more and more doors, and I will feel like I belong.

PART 1

Hunger

Hunger (noun) | A feeling of discomfort or weakness caused by lack of food, coupled with the desire to eat.

I remember the first day I question my hunger. It's Tuesday, Pasta Night. I am twelve years old and watching my mom cook. She stirs the simmering RAGÚ sauce as the Barilla penne boils in another pot. The air is full of the aromas of roasting garlic and sweet tomatoes. My stomach rumbles as garlic sizzles with the onion. I recognize this as hunger.

"Set the table, Alz, please," my mom says as she looks over her shoulder while stirring the sauce.

I place pasta bowls, silverware, and napkins at everyone's seat. When I finish my task, I look back at my mother. Her brow is furrowed. Somehow I've done something wrong.

"Oh, I don't need a big bowl," she says.

Now I feel even more confused. I'm used to us always eating from our large white pasta bowls. I don't understand why she only wants a small green bowl for a side dish. Did something happen to her that she doesn't want pasta? I can't wrap my mind around this decision since Pasta Night means we all eat pasta.

"Well, what are you going to eat your pasta in?" I ask her.

"Oh no, sweetie, not tonight. I'm not that hungry." She sounds nonchalant.

My mom sometimes tells me about tricks to squeeze in my belly to ensure I have a flat stomach. Now I wonder if her lack of hunger is a new way for her to maintain her flat stomach. I want to ask her why she isn't hungry, but instead I just accept her answer, despite not understanding how someone cannot be hungry. We gather as a family at the table—my dad, my sister, me, and my mom. Mom always serves herself last. We all have bowls of pasta except for Mom. She serves herself a small bowl of green beans to accompany her salad.

I watch my mom eat her green beans as I begin to eat my pasta. I cannot comprehend why she doesn't want more. *If my mom isn't that hungry, then why am I so hungry? Why does my stomach rumble so loudly? Why do I have a big bowl? Should I be hungry? Is it wrong to be hungry?*

The questions pile up. The concerns increase. Maybe my body is against me. Maybe it's causing me to crave something I shouldn't, to have desires that aren't true. If my mom is just eating green beans, why don't I just want green beans? Perhaps the rumbling in my body is a lack of willpower.

I start to feel a deep desire to never experience that rumbling in my stomach again. My mind feels dizzy with questions. *Why can't I be like my mom? Why can't I stop being hungry? When I grow up, will I finally stop being hungry?*

Body Awareness

I stand at the James River in a blue swimsuit in between Lauren, my sister, and my Aunt Aimee. The breeze brushes against my skin. My mom interrupts this sensation by snapping a picture of me and my sister. My sister is tall and thin, wearing a pink halter-top bikini and a seashell necklace. Her body is the perfect fit for her low-rise bikini. I look down at my protruding belly in my one-piece swimsuit. I long to be like my tall, tan, thin sister in so many ways, but I especially crave to have a body like hers.

We play in the river, skipping rocks and wading in the current. My body isn't my primary focus while I play, yet I'm still aware of my belly, how my thighs touch one another, and how my large feet are almost too big for kids' shoes.

At ten years old, I know my body isn't normal. Doctors have said I'm in the highest percentile for height and even larger for weight. They call me "big-boned."

I don't want to topple over every boy in my grade. I don't want to cry in the Limited Too dressing room, perturbed that I'm ten years old and wearing a size 14/16. I have thousands of thoughts, many about my body, running through my mind. I don't want to be preoccupied with my size. But I am, and I think I've always been that way.

Running Minds

My mind doesn't just race with thoughts about my body. My mind is like a broken music box. No matter how hard I try to close it, the music will not turn off. I'm continually running through fields of puzzles, questioning the meaning of life, counting numbers, and analyzing every situation I've been in or may encounter in the future. I don't know silence.

I'm five years old, sitting on top of a closed toilet seat. I'm waiting to start afternoon kindergarten. In the mornings, I explore the playground of my mind. I focus my attention on our small bathroom corridor, and I find names for each green and white tile. My journal sits on my lap, my pen in hand, and I begin to write lesson plans, create math problems, and craft speeches. I call on each tile to ask them what they think heaven is. Tile One, let's call her Gabby, says, "Heaven is a beautiful place where there is no pain." Tile Two, Sam, says he thinks "heaven is where there is no cancer and where Jesus can hug you and sing with you." I take notes as I craft the speech I will give to my mom before we leave for school about the meaning of heaven. Together, the tiles and I contemplate whether there is a heaven and, if so, who gets to go there.

That afternoon on the school playground, I ask my classmates what they think about heaven. They just want to play tag and hot lava; they have no interest in my ideas about heaven. In my mind alone, I continue to ponder this question with my tiles, my journals, and with the adults at family parties, feeding my desire to constantly learn.

When I'm seven years old, I can't sleep. Earlier that day, my teacher, Mrs. Kowalski, gave me a booklet of logic puzzles to take home. Before bed I turn on my reading light underneath the sheets, so my parents can't tell I'm up past my bedtime. I get through three puzzles, but on the fourth I'm stumped. Still, I'm determined to figure out this logic puzzle before I fall asleep.

Every ounce of my being tightens as I struggle to solve this puzzle. My heart races. Anger rushes through my body as I toss and turn and punch the pillow. Since I can't figure it out, I close the book in defeat, turn off my light, and try to go to sleep.

Yet my mind continues to churn, picturing the different scenarios in my head. If Annie likes red and is a teacher, and Joe likes blue but doesn't like yard work, then Sam must like green, and if he also doesn't like yard work, then. . . . The thoughts speed around in my head until I can't escape my mind and scream for my mom as panic takes over my body.

She rushes into the room, nervous that maybe this time it's an emergency, but soon she realizes it's just another sleepless night for my restless mind.

"Sweetie, what's wrong tonight?" she calmly asks.

"I can't figure out the math problem!" I shout.

"Math problem? What math problem?"

"We did logic problems in class today, and I was very frustrated that I couldn't figure out the problem on the first try. I asked Mrs. Kowalski if I could bring five problems home, so I could practice and get better for next time. Now I can't figure this one out, and I'm just so frustrated," I explain.

"Shh, Alzie, it's okay. You can figure out the problem tomorrow."

But I don't want to wait until tomorrow; I want to figure it out now. Slowly, the soothing scratches bring me to sleep, but the moment my alarm sounds in the morning, I bring out my logic puzzles to complete while eating cereal and drinking a glass of OJ, determined to figure them out. What would it be like if my head wasn't full of math problems to solve, ideas to develop, and a never-ending pressure to learn? How would I feel if I were silently safe inside my own head?

Ordinarily Nothing

At a very young age, I learn this belief: Average is unacceptable. Anyone can be average, but I was put into this world to be great. If I'm ordinary, I'm wasting away my life. Teachers, coaches, and mentors encourage this flame by telling me I can be exceptional. As I grow up, I hard-code this belief into my brain.

This root belief fuels so much:

- Average students receive grades below an A.
- Average and below-average players belong on B teams.
- Average actors are cast in supporting roles.
- Average dreamers only have bleak dreams.
- Average learners are in non-advanced classes.
- Average athletes don't break physical fitness test records.
- Below-average humans procrastinate.
- Average kids are happy to engage in kid conversations.
- Second place doesn't matter because it's not first.
- If I'm average, I don't matter.

This belief also has branches:

- If I'm not exceptional, I'm not worthy.
- I'm destined for something great, so I need to be great.
- I'm wasting away my life if I'm not dreaming big dreams.
- If I don't put action behind my dreams, I'm merely taking up space.
- If I'm average at anything, I'm ordinary.
- If I'm ordinary, I'm nothing.

Too Muchness

We're in Mexico on a family vacation. I'm nine years old, and my sister, Lauren, is a teenager. She is painfully shy in contrast to my larger-than-life personality. She refuses to speak to waiters or order for herself, so I gladly order for her at every meal. This dynamic carries on beyond vacations. Growing up, I took up so much of the space that my sister slowly faded into the background. I yearned to be the center of attention; I did not let her be seen. I existed in complete contrast to my sister, whose thin body and shyness were not too much—she was what a young girl was supposed to be.

I'm too loud. Every day I hear warnings to use my inside voice.

I'm too controlling. I always need to be the leader of the pack, the planner of the group.

I'm too much of a goody two-shoes. I always sit in the front of the class with my hand confidently raised to answer the teacher's question.

I'm too intense. I ask for extra homework. I'm the first to arrive and the last to leave.

I'm too happy. I smile too much. I'm told it's not normal.

I take up too much space. Large bodies do not win over boys, score goals, or win track meets.

I'm just too much. I'm too much for this world.

"Allyson loves life and has so much energy, but sometimes it's a bit much for the other students."

You will not fit in by being too much; you will not keep friends by being too much; you will never get a boy to like you by being too much; the world will not accept you if you are too much.

So you chip away at yourself.

Instead of being too loud, try to use your inside voice or stop talking.

Instead of trying too hard, continue to write, but hide your As.

Instead of being a goody two-shoes, sneak out to hook up with boys.

Instead of being too intense, when you're around the popular kids, pretend you don't care.

Instead of being too happy, wear a mask to hide both your smile and your pain.

Instead of taking up too much space, dedicate yourself to finding ways to shrink.

Instead of being too much, aim to be not enough.

You will fit in when you are average; you will fit in when you are quieter; you will fit in when you are mean; you will fit in when you are small; you will fit in when you learn that being not enough is better than being too much.

Running with My Dad

My dad wears a white cutoff T-shirt and a backwards cap. It's a Saturday morning. I sit next to him as we both lace up our shoes. I'm a curious eight-year-old witnessing his daily exercise routine. He packs his black, smelly gym bag. I pack my lime green one.

"Ready to go, buddy?"

"Sure, Daddy!"

We head to the Westlake Rec Center, our neighborhood's meeting place filled with mostly white, affluent families. Older kids, twelve and up, exercise upstairs in a room called the DEN. Since I'm not allowed there yet, I grab a basketball and begin to dribble, not particularly well, but moving nonetheless. My dad runs laps on the upstairs track as I practice my basketball skills down below. On that day when I see my dad running, I stop dribbling. I don't want to play basketball. I want to run. I leave the ball under a bleacher and head upstairs to the track area, meeting him as he completes a lap.

"Hey, Dad, can I join you? I want to run a mile with you."

I didn't know what that truly meant. It just seemed like the right thing to say.

"Sure, buddy—but you know twelve laps is a mile, right? Let's see if you can make three to start."

I nod, yet in the back of my mind, I know I want to run a mile. I'm not going to stop at three laps. How hard could this running thing be?

My dad, fast by nature, smiles at me and says, "Don't worry, I'll run them with you."

So we begin, step by step, one foot in front of the other. My heart pounds, and I can feel my lungs releasing each breath. I remind myself I have done this before. I have run for basketball and soccer. Yet, when I run for those sports, it's all toward a goal—I run to shoot the ball, to guard a fast forward from scoring, to do conditioning drills, or most often, as punishment when our coach is angry with our performance. I have never run for the sake of running.

As my heart beats faster, I feel exhilarated. It reminds me of times when I received an A+ on a paper or performed on stage in a play. But this time, it's painful and exhilarating all at once. There is something so thrilling about the pounding in my chest. I have never felt so alive.

I finish the twelve laps. My determination and drive power each step.

I don't know how long it takes me to finish, but none of this matters. I see a look in my dad's eyes that I recognize as pride.

"High five, you just ran a mile! Way to go!"

After that Saturday, our routine changes. I no longer watch my dad run on the track above me. I run with him. We circle the indoor track in the winter, and we run around our neighborhood in the Cleveland summer heat. Each time, I feel the familiar pounding, that painful and exhilarating aliveness.

Running is the one place where I find solace from my continually racing mind. The runner's high quiets all my questions. When I run, I no longer need to worry about why cancer exists in this world, what new math problems I should try to solve, if I would ever make the A team in soccer, if Julie would like me today, why my body isn't as small as Halle's, or if heaven is real. I learn to let go of the thoughts that seem never to end. Instead, I experience every part of my body: the sweat dripping down my cheeks and arms, the strength of my legs, going a little farther each time.

Santa Claus Bellies

I lift my pink and white striped shirt over my head and glance down at my exposed chest. It seems like overnight what used to be baby fat has turned into womanly, round grapefruits on my chest. I am eleven years old. I feel pain in my newly developed chest after running in basketball practice.

My mom says it's time we try some bras. She brings out the hand-me-down, outgrown pile of bras from my older sister. I feel wrong for needing these bras. Margaret from *Dear God, It's Me Margaret* sings phrases to increase her bust. "I must, I must, I must increase my bust." Unlike Margaret, my bust is a size B and growing.

The bell rings for lunch as the halls fill with fifth graders carelessly laughing and joking. I look in the pink mirror inside my locker and tug at my pink-and-white striped shirt. I pull it over my doughy belly. I love my pink-and-white striped shirt. Recently, I added an extra clothing item underneath it—my new bra. I stare at the locker's mirror to see if the bra is showing. It's not. But I'm still conscious of my belly—larger than Lauren's.

I grab my brown paper bag lunch, likely filled with my daily napkin lunch note, an Uncrustable, and carrots. I start to slam my locker shut as I turn around to meet Julie and Avery to walk to lunch. But instead of seeing my friends, three boys appear in my peripheral view. Before I can close the locker fully, they step in front of me, laughing in my face.

"Look. You're as fat as Santa Claus."

My jaw drops as water seeps into my eyes. I look back into the pink mirror, determined not to let them see the tears dripping down my cheeks. I wipe my face, pick up my lunch, unsure if I will even open it today, and attempt to carry on.

Mama tells me the old tale that if they tease you, it means they like you. I want to trust her. I want to believe they were only teasing. But I hear another voice too. Who would ever like a girl with a Santa Claus belly?

Behind the Dressing Room Door

Sweet and smoky scents permeate the air, like saltwater mixed with a campfire on the beach. The moment you step in and smell this, you know where you are. A tan, thin girl greets you in the moody light.

"Hey, welcome in!"

She wears body-hugging jeans, low enough to disclose glimpses of a deep V just below her flat stomach, with a tight tank top that highlights her chest. She stands with confidence and superiority, creating an unspoken desire among every passerby to be like this Abercrombie girl.

Halle is a mini version of this tall, thin, tan girl. Halle's thighs are the size of my arm. Her tiny ten-year-old body could not be more different from mine. She is a good friend, kind and soft-spoken. Halle is a normal size ten and, at times, even smaller. Her mom is a voluptuous woman whose breasts are strikingly large. My mom is tiny and flat-chested. You would think by the shape of our bodies I would belong to Halle's mom and vice versa.

My mom pulls out clothes for me that are conservative, like T-shirts without deep V necks. I am not allowed to try on Abercrombie jean shorts yet. According to my mom, they are not meant for ten-year-olds. But Halle is trying on low-cut tank tops and some ripped jean shorts. I beg my mom to try on the shorts. To avoid causing a scene, she caves. This is the first time I'm trying on adult sizes. I have no idea what a size 00, 0, 2, or 12 even means. My mom just grabs the same size as Halle; the label features two zeroes.

We take both of our selections back to the dressing rooms. I attempt to put on the shorts. I can't even button the top button. My large belly prevents any chance of zipping these double-zero shorts.

Halle's mom calls out from outside the door, "Girls! Let me see how they look."

I can't walk out of this dressing room. I can't even wear normal-size clothes at Limited Too, and now I'm wearing sizes larger than what a young woman would wear. I look in the mirror with my unzipped pants and the tight pink shirt that emphasizes my large breasts. My heart races. I can't move.

I meet the mirror's gaze in complete and utter disapproval. I hear Halle's dressing room door close and a clamor of "Ooh, you look great! Those fit you so well." I'm envious and frustrated, wishing I could trade places with Halle. Life could be so much better if only I didn't take up so much space.

My mom calls out to me.

My throat catches, and with a broken voice, all I say is, "It didn't work." Mom knocks and asks to come in.

I don't let her see me. I can't let anyone see that I'm broken by my body. So instead, I take one more look at my large body, pull the jean shorts off, fold them, put on my happy mask, and walk out the dressing room door. I smile at Halle, telling her I'm glad the clothes worked out for her, and maybe another time I can come back to try on something else.

Behind the dressing room door, the mirror will keep my secrets: I am not small enough; I take up too much space; I am wrong, wrong, wrong.

Athlete (I Am Not)

Soccer

Natalie dribbles the ball up the field, her tiny thighs the size of my calves. I start on the B team; my natural talent was not good enough for the A team. I watch the A team practice from afar, and every ounce of my being wants to be a part of that team. The B team, a.k.a. "the Blast," is not, in fact, a blast.

The B team is for those who are average and unexceptional. The A team is for athletes. At fourth-grade tryouts, I finally make the A team. However, as the newbie on the team, I need to prove myself. So I show up early, stay late; I use my determination to prove I deserve a spot on the team.

"What if you try goalie or maybe defense?" my new coach suggests. "I don't think you'll be fast enough for midfield or forward."

I hate goalie, and defense is for the large, slow girls. I want to be the tiny, fast girl in front. I want to feel the rush of scoring a goal. I want to be the best; I want to matter. Defense is not where I want to be. Scoring goals matters.

I will get quicker. I will outwork any person on this field. Laser-focused, my drive pushes me forward. I will become the athlete I am not.

Swimming

My eyes are fixed on the end of the lane; I will be the first to touch the wall. I put my goggles on. I look at the other six-year-olds next to me, my competition for the day. We step up to the block, the announcer commanding us to our places.

"On your marks, get set, go."

We jump, my body propelling forward. If I swim my race, I can win. I move gracefully, fast: stroke right, stroke left, kicking to the rhythm of my arms as I pull the water along swiftly. I'm the first to the wall. When it's time for me to rise from the water, I'm beaming with a fist in the air.

Every morning I wake up at 6:00 a.m. for swim practice. I started swimming in my neighborhood pool at two years old. Family and friends said I was like a little fish. And I did feel like a fish in water. There was something so natural about swimming—like coming home.

At each meet, I collect at least one ribbon. The ribbons prove my worthiness. During one meet, I'm asked to be part of my sister's relay team. One of the girls has dropped out, and they need a last-minute substitute. Even though I'm four years younger, I'm convinced my drive alone has won me many ribbons and will help me win this race too. But as we begin, I quickly realize my ambition will not bring us victory. The competition is fast, and as soon as I get in the water, I lose any lead our team has. I let them down.

My mom reminds me I was swimming with older girls, and I did my best. But, in my mind, age doesn't matter. I've disappointed everyone. I am not quick enough. I will not swim next season. My ribbons are now meaningless. Regardless of my drive, I'm still not enough. I'm not an athlete.

Softball

I try softball for one season. It's filled with downtime and waiting. A pitcher makes or breaks the game. I don't know why my sister enjoys it so much. Each time she gets up to the mound, she winds up and throws with such speed and precision. She doesn't practice in the evening and always refuses to go to the batting cages with my dad at night. I throw the ball with him when he asks. Lauren is able to just show up and excel. I am the opposite. Although I practice, I can neither coordinate my swing, nor pump myself up enough to learn it. To me, softball is too slow and boring. I'm only inspired when I see my sister step onto the field. She is the athlete—I don't even have a shot.

Track

I'm in sixth grade performing the physical fitness test. I attempt to make it to the opposite side of the gym before I hear the next beep. If that beep occurs and I'm not over to the other side, I must start again. If I can't make it to the other side before I hear the next beep, or if I do not start again before the following beep, I am eliminated. The last person standing wins, or at least that's the way my brain sees it.

I eye my competition to see who I'm up against. My best friend, LoLo, is not in my class this year. My next true competitor is Grace, who is small and mighty. But as the beeps continue, quickness becomes less important than drive. Under no circumstance will I drop out until I am the only one left. I will be the best. As the beeps go on, my chest burns, and my legs feel increasingly heavy. Still, I continue to run. My mind is made up.

The gym teacher is also the seventh-grade track coach. After class that day, he pulls me aside to compliment me on my determination and ask if I'm coming out for track next year. Instantly, I think of LoLo and her quickness. I tell myself, if she were in this class, she would have beat me. She has a natural ability for speed, winning almost every race. So I tell him, "No, running for me is joyful. I don't want to add competition to it." But in reality, my doubt blocks me from even stepping up to the starting line. If I can't be the best, why try?

Basketball

Every Saturday afternoon, I go to the Westlake Rec Center for one-on-one clinics with Coach Keneally. We practice drills: dribbling in and out of the legs, around the world with quick, low dribbles as we walk up and down the court. My brow furrows, my eyes squint, and the sound of the ball bouncing on the court keeps me focused. If I get these drills down, I'll know I'm getting better each day.

Corinne enters the court and swishes the ball on every shot. With a flick of her wrist, she lands each shot precisely in the hoop. We play a round of knockout; her perfect accuracy knocks me out each time. I am determined to play again and again until I finally win . . . by happenstance or by skill, I still don't know.

My dad and I play horse and one-on-one after dinner on crisp Midwest summer nights. Once the sun goes down, the sky is illuminated by our outdoor court light and summertime lightning bugs. I cherish these nights in the summer air when my dad lets me win almost every one-on-one game. It's like running together. These are moments for us to connect and for me to prove I can use my drive and persistence to excel.

I consider travel basketball, yet they assure me I am behind the curve to make the best team. So I trade in my basketball shoes for ankle braces and focus my vision on volleyball. I'm still not an athlete. And if I have any chance of being one, volleyball will be my best bet.

Volleyball

I jump up to the net, sprint back to the ten-foot line, watch the hitter's arm as she tips the ball, watch the ball hit my arms as I dig the ball, sprint back to the ten-foot line, watch the set, jump into the air, feel the ball on my palm, and slam it down to the other side of the court. The constant movement, swift feet, high-fives, chants, determination, and teamwork all leave me on a constant, sweat-dripping high.

Volleyball is 90 percent mental and 10 percent skill, according to my coaches. The moment I "get in my head," mistakes seem to happen—balls served out, hits going into the net, second-guessing who would get the ball. Yet, when I let everything go and just play, we all move on the court in synergy. When I let go of needing it to be perfect, everything somehow clicks. There is no need to always be the fastest or smallest. The strength in my arms and in my powerful legs propels me farther into the air.

Each point in the game is like a mental high, knowing each point is a team effort, hearing the cheers erupt every time we succeed. Volleyball teaches me how to lead, how to get out of my head and into my body. I learn how quickly energy can be built and how just as quickly it can be stripped away. It shows me how we can lift each other up, how no one person can be a superhero, and how to push through, moment to moment.

I played competitive volleyball for eight years. It was my closest attempt at being an athlete.

Coach Kim and Mental Toughness

The ball drops on the court beside me. Sweat drips down my cheeks. My white shirt is drenched. I dive for ball after ball in the Pit of Hell drill, though I will never win. Balls are thrown, balls are slammed, balls are placed just barely out of reach to land on all parts of the court as I attempt to touch each ball before it hits the gray plastic floor. Once I touch thirty balls in a row without a single mistake, I am released from the drill.

I run from side to side, craving to please Coach Kim. Fifteen minutes later, my breath is heavy, and my legs shake with exhaustion. I am at ball twenty-eight. After barely digging a ball up from the back left corner of the court, I see Coach Kim tip a ball barely over the net into the top right corner. I imagine this ball is a best friend falling from a high-rise building who I'm desperately trying to save. I step with my right foot, then left, then lunge forward toward the nearly landed ball. My fingertips reach out and almost graze the ball, but it's too late. The ball hits the plastic floor. The Pit of Hell defeats me once again. Burn marks quickly appear on my skin—my body's proof of my valiant effort. But it's not enough.

I look up with pleading eyes at Coach Kim. Her curly brown hair bounces in complete opposition to the fire fuming from her eyes. I attempt to look away, hoping my new burn marks show the attempt I made to save the ball.

Coach Kim jumps down from the box. "Get in here! Huddle up! Now!" she screeches, her high-pitched voice reverberating off the ceiling panel and open gym walls.

All twelve of us rush over to her command.

Her piercing eyes glance around the circle of nervous girls who only want to win her approval. Her nose scrunches up as I can feel her vicious eyes pierce my soul.

"Ha, is that what you call volleyball? Is that really your best attempt?"

My lip quivers as I see the *No pain, No gain* sign plastered on the white wall.

Don't cry, don't cry, don't cry.

"Are you going to answer me?"

I attempt to answer her, but it takes every ounce of strength to focus on not crying. I know that if I even try to open my mouth, no words will come out—only water will trickle from my eyes.

"Nothing? Well, after that performance, you don't deserve to be on this team. You deserve to be down the toilet, in the sewer, filled with shit."

"And you, Tiff," pointing at our setter standing next to me who was in the Pit just before I entered, "you don't even belong on this earth. You belong on Jupiter or somewhere in space where no one has to deal with you."

We all stand there frozen and silent, but our silence only infuriates Coach Kim.

"Really? You all are usually so talkative, and now you have nothing to say? Fine. Get on the line. Suicides. Now. We will run until practice is over or until one of you pukes."

Don't cry, don't cry, don't cry.

I line up with my fellow soldiers and begin to run. *No pain, no gain* creates mental toughness, they say. We run and run and run until Tiff finally pukes. Despite Coach Kim's promise, when she sees Tiff's puke, she becomes even more infuriated. So we don't stop. We continue to run. We run until five minutes after practice was supposed to end. Coach Kim blows her whistle as she looks at us with disgust.

"You're done. Get out of here. Come back tomorrow ready to do this all over again."

I run to my bag, avoiding any teammates as my body is filled with disgust and unworthiness. My mom waits for me in our silver minivan. Before she can ask how practice is, I begin to kick the minivan's windshield uncontrollably from the front passenger seat. My body shakes. I keep kicking and screaming, wishing my screams would release the pain that rushes through my body.

My mom attempts to touch my thigh, to squeeze my hand, to somehow bring me back. As a passionate and emotional child, she has seen me get angry before but nothing to this degree. Eventually she reaches over and collects my entire shaking body in her arms. I still scream. I'm done. I'm defeated. But at Coach Kim's command, I go back the next day, get on the line to finish our suicides, and become "mentally tough."

My Search for "Normal"

It's a warm summer weekend, and I recently got a two-piece from Limited Too. The swimsuit has padding, and I'm hyperaware of the way my body looks compared to my tiny, fit friends. We are going to Julie's cabin in Port Clinton with the popular crowd. They're known for flirting with boys, playing spin the bottle, skinny dipping, and knowing what Mike's Hard Lemonades are. I fall asleep first.

My sleepover bag is perfectly packed to hide the sports bras I've recently acquired. My stomach is filled with knots. What if they discover my secret of already needing a sports bra? It's only nine o'clock, and they are just beginning to play truth or dare. Whoever falls asleep first gets pranked, they warn. I try my best to stay awake, yet my eyelids get heavy as I nod off.

I fall asleep on the couch, and they continue to play truth or dare. I do not know what truths were shared or what dares were taken; I do know that when I wake up at 8:00 a.m. to go to my bag, it's no longer how I had packed it. *No, they could not have found it. No. No. No.*

I frantically tear my bag apart to find everything besides the one item I dreaded they would find. I sprint out of my room, screaming and crying.

"Where is it? Where'd you put it? What did you guys do?"

"You gotta find it. It's part of the game," Julie says.

Now I'm fuming with anger. "No. I will not find it. Just tell me. NOW! Please just tell me."

"Just check the freezer," LoLo shouts, as Julie glares at her.

I run to the freezer and find my sports bra frozen. The sobs turn into shrieks as I take the ice block of a bra out of the freezer and chuck it at the group of girls who all stare back at me, saying nothing.

"Julie, where is your mom? I need her to call my mom. I want to go home."

"Jeez, calm down. It was just a silly prank. Maybe you shouldn't be the first one to fall asleep next time." Julie laughs.

The prank highlighted how not okay my body was. How it would be so much better to freeze off my boobs instead of having bras that could be frozen. How I should be like a normal eleven-year-old with a thin body and tiny boobs.

Slut

"Thank you, baby. That's the best gift I could have ever received. I love you."

Is that what this sinking, gut-wrenching, disgusted feeling is? Love? The pit of my stomach fills with nauseous nothingness and an overwhelming feeling that this is wrong, so wrong. I stare at the games and toys around me. They remind me of the innocence of what I should be doing at twelve years old. I should be playing board games, not the games in the mind of a fast-paced boy. I stare at the green sending dial on my flip phone as I pull my baby-doll blue shirt and sports bra back down over my too-large chest. A moment later, I look down at his words lit up on my screen. My hands violently shake as I delete the picture, attempting to erase the sinking feeling of endless shame. The gift is only for his eyes, so he claims. The gift shows I am the best girlfriend, so he claims.

It's a Monday morning when I walk into the lunchroom, a place that also serves as our meeting place before the first bell. I sit with the popular girls at the table in the top right corner of the room. We nickname ourselves "the clique" after the most recent book series we all read.

The closer I get to the table, the more I feel something is off. I sit down at the open seat, and all of the clique moves down to the other side of the lunch bench, blatantly ignoring me. It's as if I am a ghost, and they can't even see me.

I ask them how their weekend was. No response. I then ask them what's wrong. No response. I run to the bathroom, convinced they must know about the gift I sent this weekend. Their silent treatment continues for three months, but it includes two short intermissions.

On a random Tuesday, I sit alone at a picnic table. Anthony asks me if I want to smoke from a bong. I don't know what a bong is, so I politely decline. A minute later, Austin asks me to come to the four-corner court because someone has a surprise for me.

Maybe this is when the girls will apologize, and we will all go back to being friends, and everything will be normal, but no, I am immensely mistaken. The clique surprises me, instead, by taunting me with their rendition of the hit song "Superstar" by Lupe Fiasco.

"You are what you say you are, a porn star.

Have no fear, Brad's here.

Let your mountains show,

'Cause everyone knows."

As the song ends, the girls erupt in laughter while I run into school, tears rushing down my face. I want to vomit, to not exist, to be anywhere but here in this school or on this earth.

The next week during math class, the whole class is silent during our homework time. Homework time is usually filled with minimal actual homework and mostly loud chatter. Today is different. Amid the silence, Nadine counts to three.

Then in unison, a resounding "Ally's a slut" fills the air.

My jaw drops, and I sprint out of the room and into the bathroom. Mr. Shill, the middle school math teacher who witnessed the chorus, enlists Mrs. Rome, our guidance counselor, to lure me out of the bathroom despite every part of me wanting to hide in the stall. Mrs. Rome states she is here to provide me with some "help."

I soon learn she has called my parents about the picture because my supposedly worried "friends" decided to tell Mrs. Rome about the incident, claiming they were deeply concerned for my well-being.

I didn't know that friends who care about you also tee-pee your pool, fill it with mulch, and carve the word "BOOBS" into your deck. That picture of me is now out there for everyone's pleasure and mockery. My body is no longer mine.

First Touch

It's a winter afternoon at the rec center pool. I tell my mom I'm meeting up with friends to hang out and play basketball. My stomach is filled with knots, knowing this is a lie. I'm not going to meet friends. I'm seeing Brad. We plan to go swimming. I wear my rainbow polka dot bikini from Limited Too.

It's a month after I sent him "the picture." When I asked him about why the picture got out, he blamed it on his friend Chris. He claimed Chris stole his phone, saw it, and was the one who told the clique. "I promise I love you, baby, and I would never do that to you. I'm no longer friends with Chris because of it," he says. I think this is love. He's standing up for me, right? I believe him.

We begin by going down the slide and hanging in the lazy river. Soon we make our way over to the circle pool. No one else is in this pool; the lifeguard is watching all the pools from afar. A bench lines the outer rim of the circle pool, and a rope separates the pool from the diving pool. We swim in the circle pool until Brad pulls me onto the end of the bench and onto his lap. At first I feel tingly. We have only kissed a handful of times, including a few pecks and one make-out session at the movies. Making out is a big step, so I assume we will keep doing that for quite some time.

Brad wraps his arms around my waist, and then slowly his hand ventures down past my belly and toward my bikini band. I don't understand what he is doing, but I know only doctors are supposed to touch you there. His hand starts to go lower. My entire body freezes.

"What are you doing?"

"Oh, c'mon, just let me do this. It'll feel good. I know you'll like it."

I don't like it, but I don't know what to do about that. I made out with him, so maybe I'm supposed to let him touch me now. Maybe it will feel good like he says.

But it doesn't feel good. So, after a few moments of him attempting to touch me underneath my bikini bottoms, I swim away. Brad scowls and walks out of the pool.

"We're done swimming. I'm going home," he says.

I don't want to feel unwanted and unloved. I don't want to see him angry. I start to wonder if I should've just let it happen, if I should've just given in. And in that moment, I begin to think I should give my body over to a boy for his pleasure. I am merely here to comply.

PART 2

Bodies and Prey

Car Hoods

It's 8:00 p.m. on a Friday night. I'm sixteen years old, a new driver in my silver Jeep Compass. My flip phone buzzes, and I open it to see a new message from Ali.

Whatcha doing tonight?

Ali is a tall Arabic man, a junior to my sophomore status, whose eyes I can feel piercing my body in the high school hallways. He is known for getting around, and by now, so am I.

I look down at the text message, unsure of how to respond. A sinking feeling grows in my stomach though. At the same time, a sense of tingling fills my veins. I am filled with uncertainty that something about this doesn't feel right. My hands tremble. I reach for my phone.

Nm, hbu? It's not "chill" to write out full words.

Nm, wanna hang?

My heart races. Is he going to take me on a date? Maybe we will go to the movies or walk around Crocker Park mall.

Sure! Whatcha wanna do?

I'm at Moe's place. We're having some people over. You should swing by.

Swing by? My head spins. What does that mean? I don't know, but I already said yes and don't want to look like I'm not cool by backing out.

K cool—I'll be there in 15.

I tell my mom I'm going to June's to hang. I know she won't question this. Her mom and mine talk but not often enough for my cover to be blown. My hands are sweaty as my heart races faster with the excitement of being sixteen and wanted by an "older boy."

I get to Moe's place at 9:00 p.m.; it's pitch-black outside with streetlights lighting the way. I send a casual "here" text and see the door open. Ali walks out in black skinny jeans, white sneakers, and a light purple T-shirt.

"Should I come inside?" I ask, walking toward him.

"Ah, no. I needed a break from the guys. Let's just hang out here."

"Okay, what do you want to do?"

"Let's just hang on the hood of your car and get to know one another a little better."

Before I know it, we are sitting on top of the hood of my car, one of his hands on top of mine, pushing it down his pants, the other on my double-D breast. I begin to move my hand like I have been taught to do. My hands for his pleasure. I continue as his eyes roll back, and he moans, finishing within minutes.

A sigh of relief escapes from his body as his hands move down to my pants. He undoes my button and goes lower. My whole body tenses, as it always does. His fingertips push deep, and all I feel is pain. I try to move away from his grasp.

"Come on," he says. "This will feel good. Don't you want to be pleasured too? I gotta return the favor."

I don't know why favors hurt this bad. I shuffle my body from side to side, attempting to escape from his grip, but his right arm holds my body down farther.

I tell him to stop, yet he does not. I don't know what will get him to stop if my words don't. I finally push his hand away and button up my jeans.

He looks at me. "That's your loss, I guess. I'm really good at fingering." With that, he jumps off the hood of my car and walks back toward the house.

I am left in the black of the night, alone. I get back into my car and begin to cry. And then the voice in my head reminds me I have no reason to cry.

I touched him. I let him touch me. I chose to be his prey.

Puke

We lay on Sam's bed, as Luke and Alyssa make out upstairs. My shirt is off. The prized "giant titties" are here for his groping pleasure. We start the day with my mockery of sharing that I have no gag reflex. It's a casual little fun fact to share about myself. Tonight proves different.

He holds my head down. I suck his penis as the back of his hand cradles the back of my head. The cradling turns into a firm hold. Something about this feels different as my head is pushed farther and farther down. I attempt to reach up for air again and again and again, but I can't seem to release from his grip. I can feel it coming up. I try to release my head as water fills my eyes, yet his grip becomes stronger than ever. I cannot release from his grip, so instead, I vomit. Everywhere.

I lift up as he looks at me horrified. I'm filled with dread, and I begin to profusely apologize.

"Um, that's disgusting," he says. I don't know what to do. I'm frozen.

He runs to the bathroom to clean up as I rapidly whip my shirt back on, my mind spinning with shame. I don't know my shirt is on backwards until I get home later that night and my mom asks me why my shirt is inside out and where I've been. I use June as an excuse, but it doesn't work this time.

"Allyson, you were not at June's. I know that for a fact. And why is your shirt so disheveled? What is going on?"

My mind fills with so many other thoughts that I don't even care if my mom is mad at me. "I'm fine!" I shout, and I run upstairs.

The next day the entire basketball team knows how inaccurate my little fun fact is. I chose this. I went. I gave him the blow job. After all, isn't that all my body and mouth are here for—to be a play toy for whichever boy I'm prey to that night? My body, his pleasure. I chose to be his play toy.

Escape

I run. I run as fast as I can. I run down his apartment stairs into my car and drive away. This is it. I am done feeling worthless. I am done being a toy for men. I can't do this anymore.

Sixty seconds prior, his body is on top of mine. The weight of his body presses down, a tale as old as time. He unzips my pants with one hand as he unzips his with the other. He takes out his penis and moves it closer to enter me. But this time I know. I know I don't want to have sex. I don't want to be under this boy. I go to lift up, but his grip remains strong, and his body weighs heavily on mine. I try to lift up again; he continues to hold me down.

"I don't want to do this."

"C'mon, just let it happen. It'll feel good."

This time I know it won't. I use every ounce of strength in me and push him off. I grab my bag, my keys, and I run. And yet again in my head, the thoughts come.

I chose this. I went. I kissed him. After all, isn't that all my body is here for—to be a play toy for whichever boy I am prey to that night? Yet this time, a part of me wants the answer to be no.

When I run out of his apartment, my breath heavy, hands shaking, a small part of me is reminded of what it feels like to move my body just for me. In this movement, a faint voice tells me it's time to reclaim my body. It's time to stop letting boys feed off my body. It's time to move again just for me—that is how I will gain control.

The Voice of ED

I hear a whisper in my head that's similar to the one I heard on the night I ran out of Nick's apartment. The voice has a low raspy tone similar to my own. This voice is slightly different though—a bit lower and more direct. Because the voice sounds similar to mine, I begin to accept it as my own.

"Trust me, if you start to listen to me, you will take back control. No man will ever hurt you, and you will never be prey to a man again." The voice is direct. At this point, it doesn't yet consume all of me. As I drive to the gym for morning workouts, the voice encourages me to lift a little longer and track my workouts. My muscles feel strong as I do two more reps, confidence growing as my muscles do too.

When I go to eat, the voice encourages me to be sure I am eating healthy and "clean." I no longer grab the curly fries and chocolate chip cookie for lunch. Instead, I eat my bag of carrots and rolled turkey, unsatisfied, yet honoring the voice that assures me this is for my own good, my own strength, my own health. I believe that honoring this voice is an act of self-love.

The more I listen to the voice, the stronger it becomes. Instead of just affirming I'm getting healthy and strong, it affirms this is an act of willpower. The more miles I run and the more times I say no to Mitchell's ice cream, the more willpower and determination I have. Willpower and determination will help me fit through the right doors.

Quickly the voice not only becomes stronger but also louder and more ominous. Every step I take, every decision I make, the voice is there by my side. The voice becomes so loud that I begin to lose my own, as this one dominates any other thoughts I have. The voice not only speaks at the gym and when I eat, but when I look in the mirror and when I try to talk to LoLo. I pretend to hear her when all I can truly hear is the voice.

Soon nothing is ever enough for the voice. The voice will remind me sparingly that all the exercise and food rules are for my health and willpower and, instead, tells me more that I'm not doing enough—I'm not strong enough, fit enough, listening enough.

"You need to eat less. You need to run more. You are still fat. You will still be desirable to men. Don't you want to lose your boobs, so you're no longer prey? Don't you want to be small enough, so you can be fast? Don't you want to be the best?"

I try to appease the voice—to eat less, to work more, to shrink, to gain the voice's approval. But the more I try, the louder and more demeaning the voice becomes. I am determined to win the voice's approval. I follow the voice more closely each day, believing it will be the one to finally make me exceptional.

The 17 Day Diet

In 2010 someone by the name of Dr. Mike Moreno releases a book called *The 17 Day Diet*. This diet claims to be a "simple plan that targets both belly fat and visceral fat and produces fast results that last!" He claims it's "a revolutionary new weight-loss program that activates your *skinny gene*, so you burn fat day in and day out." The 17 Day Diet consists of four cycles that instantly catch my attention: accelerate, activate, achieve, arrive.

As a sixteen-year-old, I don't understand what a skinny gene is, or what metabolic restarting does, or why you need to flush sugar from your body. I do know that anything that may help me get rid of any remnants of my Santa Claus belly and double-D chest is a plan I want to follow.

"I just want to try it," I tell my mom.

Throughout my sixteen years, my mom has tried multiple diets, but it seems nothing works for her either. My mom is not a large woman. She goes for regular walks, does her Pilates videos daily, attends the rec center classes, and has a healthy diet. However, she is eager to rid herself of her "elephant arms."

Barnes and Noble is one of our favorite destinations together. We often spend hours perusing the various bookshelves, discovering new stories, and getting lost in the worlds between two covers. Today, though, we are looking for *The 17 Day Diet* book. There will be no browsing; we are on a mission to "get healthier." That is what we tell ourselves, but in my mind, I want to be as small as I can be.

"This is something we can try together," my mom says, pointing to the Week Four chapter description. "Especially because it says we can enjoy our favorite foods eventually."

I agree to anything that may help me lose volume in my belly and chest. I determine that without my double-D boobs, boys will not like me, so I must find a way to get rid of my chest, as I no longer want boys to like me. In the back of the book, Dr. Moreno provides a grocery list of foods, including lean proteins and tons of veggies. This guide tells us to drink hot lemon water in the mornings before we consume any food and eat a few portions of chicken and veggies daily. After purchasing the book, we go to our local grocery store to gather the ingredients for "Phase One."

On the first morning, I start with my hot lemon water and pack some rolled turkey and a handful of carrots for lunch. My group of six or so friends asks why I am not getting my usual cookies or curly fries. I tell them I am trying something new with my mom. I spare them the details, nervous about what judgment may follow. No one asks any questions. All of us girls understand diets are a way of life.

My weight starts to drop rapidly. My mom's weight does not fall off as fast.

Soon I notice my clothes are now too big for me. I feel more energetic, have a clearer mind, and most importantly, I start to get a glimpse of what smallness feels like. This is what I've been waiting for.

I stop during Phase One: Accelerate. I want to go fast, and this phase speeds along like lightning, so I stay. In the future phases, they add higher calorie days. But after doing a week of Phase One, I don't want to consume any calories higher than what I have been consuming; doing so seems like walking right back into a trap that won't help me reach my goals.

I learn about meal prepping and the importance of weighing food. As soon as I find out about scales, I convince my mom to go to our local Bed Bath & Beyond and buy one for me. Simply measuring out portion sizes with a measuring cup is not good enough; I need precision.

Day by day, week by week, I stay on this diet, and it becomes dizzyingly intense. I eliminate foods off my list of what I'm allowed to eat. Something else has to be measured. My Google searches tell me too much salt can lead to swelling, and sugar is the ultimate enemy. If I want to lose weight, then I must do cardio every day. Flat stomachs are made in the kitchen. Red meat will cause cholesterol problems. Any potatoes except for sweet potatoes are bad for me. The list is endless. The low, raspy voice tells me this plan will be the perfect path to being exceptional.

Naval Academies
and Fitness Pageants

The buildings are majestic, pristine stone. A troop of young men and women, dressed in white and navy, walk past us. Their bodies exude confidence. Every bone in my body wants to be like them. They are certain and strong. Their chests lift, their heads are raised high, and every step is meticulously in sync. I watch in awe. There is an unspoken understanding that if you are part of the Naval Academy, you've made it. I've always been a dreamer, yet this longing feels different. This is not just a pipe dream; it's a goal I am set on achieving.

Growing up, I had dreams that changed every week, sometimes every day. One day I wanted to change the world through a nonprofit. The next day I wanted to be an actress, and then the next I changed my mind and wanted to be a CEO. I was a curious, sometimes anxious child. To ease my racing mind, I always had new ideas of what would make me happy.

As I walk around the Naval Academy, the dream this time feels more permanent. This goal is terrifying yet attainable. Joining the elitist ranks is an honor that few get to say they achieved. Ultimately, this is how I will be exceptional, and selflessly exceptional at that.

"I will go here one day," I tell my mom. She smirks, knowing how often my dreams change.

"Okay, Alz. Go for it!" Despite her skepticism, my mom always supports my dreams.

Back at the hotel, I search "What does it take to get into the Naval Academy?" I start to build my plan: senator letters, fitness tests, applications, interviews, picking a sport, essays, the Summer Seminar. I reread this section.

"The Summer Seminar will introduce you to life at the Academy, where you will experience first-class academic, athletic, and professional training." This is the first step to being exceptional. I see the 25 percent acceptance rate and begin my plan to be part of that statistic. A few months later, I am notified I am part of that statistic.

"I got in! I got in! I got in!" I shiver with excitement. The next day I create a spreadsheet of everything I need to accomplish physically to have the best times at the seminar and ensure I reach my next goal of acceptance into the Academy. I call Papa Ken, who served in the Navy during the Korean War.

"Oh, Ally, I am so proud of you. You will be amazing in the Navy. You are so determined. If anyone can do it, it will be you."

My mom tells her mom who tells Papa Ray. He will not answer my call or talk to me at family gatherings. Despite also serving in the war, he is a devout evangelical Catholic who believes war is the ultimate enemy. He says I am making the worst decision of my life. By joining the Navy, I am serving the Devil.

My dad is ecstatic. His one regret in life, he claims, is never joining the military. He sets up a plan to help me. We review the spreadsheet and determine what times I need, our starting point, and the plan to reach my goals. The next day we go to the Westlake Rec Center and get to work.

We begin with the two-mile time trial on the path around the park. He brings a stopwatch, and I clock in around sixteen minutes. I know this is not good enough, but I have a baseline. "Again," I say. "Let me do it again. I know I can do better."

"We can try it again at the end," he says. "We need to get a baseline for the other tests."

I do the ball throw in the gym and realize I need to gain upper-body strength fast. I do push-ups and attempt to do pull-ups. I return to the track and run my two-mile test again. I am not proud of my base-line, but I can feel the fiery determination in every ounce of my body. I remember the person I become when my mind is set on a goal; I know my drive, consistency, and hard work will be my fuel.

We train for a week or two, going to the Westlake Rec Center every day after school. I am getting faster and stronger. My mom drives past an open garage on the way home from work and notices a woman train-ing people with battle ropes, benches, and kettlebells.

"Alzie, I think I found a spot for you to train."

We contact Annie, the trainer, tell her about my goals, do a trial workout, and I'm in. We create a plan on her whiteboard: benching goals, strength goals, speed goals, and weight goals. I have a finish line in sight, and I will stay here as long as I need to get there.

I have done conditioning and lifting for sports, but this is a whole new level. Before school, I go to Annie's gym to get my strength session in. After school and before volleyball practice, I get my run in, then go to volleyball. I begin to see the results. Annie notices my drive and potential and sees something entirely different.

I plateau slightly, so we discuss my diet.

"You know, if you're going to be committed, diet is huge. You likely are eating too much. You shouldn't be eating more than 1,700 calories. I think that will be the ultimate gamechanger."

I listen. I will do anything to get to the next level. Macros turn into calories, and I track every single morsel. The results continue to come. My double-D boobs slowly shrink; my muscles expand.

We often perform a workout of the day with a winner board of everyone who participates. These WODs are essentially CrossFit work-outs before CrossFit is "cool." The moment I see a workout posted, the posting creates a finish line where I must place first. My mental tough-ness fuels every movement and overrides any other thought.

One Thursday morning, Annie asks me a new question.

"Your drive is so strong and unlike any other sixteen-year-old or really anyone I've worked with. Have you ever heard of fitness pageants?"

I haven't heard of them before. She shows me pictures of herself at these pageants. She tells me that if I get into fitness pageants this young, I will excel. I will make so much money, and I will be so good. I go home immediately and Google what it takes to win fitness pageants. I create a plan, and slowly, the Summer Seminar dream evaporates off into the distance to be replaced by a new dream: to make money off my body, to get an actual trophy that demonstrates how I am number one.

As the training intensifies each day, I become less interested in the upcoming Summer Seminar and increasingly fascinated with the idea of the fitness pageants. While I train, I become preoccupied with this list of thoughts:

- I'll have no control over what I am eating at the Summer Seminar.
- I can't eat family style.
- How will I get in my four hours of workouts?
- Will they have Quest bars?
- How can I train for fitness pageants if I attend this?
- This will ruin me.
- This will strip me of all control.
- How do I get out of this?

A few months before the Summer Seminar starts, I tell my parents my goals have changed. I'm not interested in the Summer Seminar anymore. They are used to me changing my mind, yet this time they thought the Summer Seminar was different. To avoid any friction among us, they silently accept my decision. On the day I am supposed to leave, I go to the gym, work out for four hours, eat a Quest bar, and track every calorie and every second of movement. I do not pursue the Naval Academy dream anymore. It's no longer a dream anyway. I have set aside my dreams, so I can obsessively commit to a man named ED.

Smallness

A tiny crevice between my car and the car next to mine in the rec center parking lot makes me wonder how close I can get to the next car and still fit between the two vehicles. How much can my body shrink? How little space can I take up?

Each day I perform tests to determine my smallness.

The tests begin with a body scan in the mirror. I stand straight up and notice my legs. I have to see a fist-size gap between my thighs, or I'm not small enough. I then wrap my hands around each of my thighs. If my fingers don't touch, I'm not small enough. Next, I move up to my waist and cup my hand around my waist. If my hand doesn't form a small C, I'm not small enough. Now I bend over in the mirror. If there are any rolls at all, I'm not small enough. I then analyze my entire stomach. If I can't see every line, if my muscles aren't visible to me, I'm not small enough. I move up to my wrists and wrap my hand around my opposite wrist. My fingers can't touch, and there needs to be space between them. If there isn't, I'm not small enough. I slowly wrap my fingers continuously up my arm. The farther my fingers move up, the more worthy I become. Next, it's time to analyze my chest. If my chest is not completely flat, and if I can't see my ribs, I'm not small enough. I analyze my collarbones. If they don't distinctly protrude, I'm not small enough. I stare at my face, beginning with my cheekbones. If I can't see noticeable hollows, I'm not small enough.

I perform additional tests beyond the mirror to determine my smallness. I try on clothes. If they are larger than a size 0, I'm not small enough.

I analyze June's body—my short, fit, and naturally small five-foot, four-inch friend. If I'm not smaller than her (disregarding height), I'm not small enough. I look around any room I walk into. If I'm not the smallest person in that room, I'm not small enough.

How deeply and firmly I believe the ultimate goal in life is to minimize my presence. If I can disappear into space, then I am worthy. If I can become a shell of myself, then my life will be complete. The emptier I become, the less my mind races, and the less I am Allyson—the girl who is too much, too loud, a slut, big-boned, not special. The smaller I become, the more the world will accept me.

My Good Old FitnessPal

My handheld device tracks every dose of energy I exert and intake. I can be victorious if I'm masterful in my approach. I am determined I won't be beaten by the tiny girl with the quick feet, or my thin friend LoLo, or my sister's natural athletic ability, or a punitive coach.

The minute my alarm rings at 5:30 a.m. I'm ready to start this day's pursuit. Within five minutes, I'm dressed and out the door to the rec center for the first dose of my drug: exercise. My hands shake on the steering wheel as I crave to get to the stair stepper as fast as possible, ensuring no one else takes my prized possession. Once I arrive, I step vehemently on the StairMaster, only on level 20, and then sprint on the treadmill for three miles. It's all I can get in before school. Then I drive back home and enter my workout into MyFitnessPal. The app tracks my energy in and energy out. The more energy I expend and the less I intake, the more negative the number becomes. As I input my workout with no energy in yet, I proudly watch the negative number increase, take a seven-minute shower, then drive to school.

If I make it home with enough time, I eat my daily dose of five raspberries, two egg whites, and one tablespoon of brown rice protein powder. I scrape the tablespoon with a knife, as exact precision is critical. Before any substance is allowed into my body, it must be measured precisely and recorded to perfection. I enter these substances into MyFitnessPal as the red negative number moves closer to zero, briefly decreasing my worthiness.

At school I watch the clock anxiously until the final bell rings. My worth no longer resides in my grades, so I don't care as much about school. The perfection in me still reigns deep, so I try to focus. I still manage to get straight As and ace every exam. I don't eat lunch. Instead, I drink water and avoid food areas at all costs to ensure I'm not tempted.

During the second-to-last period, I eat my Quest bar. I record the bar before I take a bite, my worthiness shrinking again in tandem with the red negative number in MyFitnessPal. I'm even more anxious to get back to the rec center, as I must make the negative numbers high again.

As soon as the final bell rings, I briskly walk out of school, get into my car, and ensure I'm the first out of the high school parking lot. I wear a thick Under Armour long-sleeve cotton shirt, long-sleeve jacket, and an orange Clemson hoodie on top with one, sometimes two, pairs of leggings on bottom. Despite it being near seventy degrees and humid most days, I must sweat and burn as much energy as possible.

I step on the StairMaster, again only on level 20, for forty minutes. I then sprint intervals on the treadmill for thirty minutes. Next I bike on a stationary bike for a minimum of thirty minutes. My mind screams at me, "Do not stop!" As I pedal on the stationary bike, I record my StairMaster, run, and bike sessions, increasing my worth by increasing the red number.

Outside among the wet, humid air, I conduct a battle rope and kettlebell circuit for forty minutes. As I record it, the negative number grows close to negative 600 at this point. I sprint back inside and attempt to lift weights. Lifting weights gets harder as my muscles wither away. Regardless of the weight, I continue to lift. Being thin is not enough—I must also be toned.

I clock in my lift session and check my energy expenditure. If my calorie deficit is not at least negative 900, I must run more. Once it's at a minimum of negative 900, I do an abdominal circuit. The length depends on how large my Santa Claus belly feels that day. I check the clock to ensure I have been at the gym for at least three hours, sometimes four.

I know I will eat when I am home, so the expended energy must be large enough to allow for this food.

As soon as I am home, I cut up a sweet potato and weigh it to exactly fifty grams. I then cut up my chicken and measure it to two-tenths of a pound, which equates to about six small, precisely chewed bites. I put a drizzle of yellow mustard on this mixture, record it, then slowly chew my final meal of the day.

Regardless of MyFitnessPal's negative number, ED tells me I'm not worthy, I'm not enough, and I will never be enough. I must be certain my alarm is set to 5:30 a.m., go to bed, and do it all over again. *Do more* is on repeat in my mind. My day, my existence on this earth, my worthiness as a human being is determined by negative red numbers on a screen.

One More is Never Enough

Like the first breath on a cold Midwest morning, I feel a piercing sensation fill my lungs. This heaviness holds no power over my mind. My
feet throb from pounding on the treadmill as I sprint up an invisible hill.
Despite the fragility of the bones beneath my skin, my arms feel tingly
and weak when I attempt to lift weights.

None of these sensations matter. The timer ticks down on my
forty-five-minute sprint interval workout. Yesterday was forty-five minutes; today must be forty-six. If I want to be the best, I can't do the same
thing every day. I must build on each opportunity and push past any
pain, which is only a weakness in my mind that my mental toughness
can overtake.

The four-hour workout sessions do not happen overnight. Like
any new change, it's difficult at first. I wonder if it will get easier. Over
time my body and mind begin to adjust. What seemed nearly impossible before, I now embrace with ease. As I adapt, I continue to build
on the change. At times I find a balance point, yet I don't stay there.
With addiction, there is no honor in that stillness, there is no stopping.
There is only an ominous, all-consuming voice that tells me one more is
never enough.

I hear this voice throughout my workout. On the treadmill, it says
forty-five minutes is too easy. I must stay there for fifty-five minutes,
then sixty, and continue to increase every day. On the stair stepper, the
low, loud voice tells me not to stop until I feel every ounce of my body
depleted, shaking, and exhausted. During my high-intensity interval

training workouts, while covered under layers of clothing, the voice tells me I must be drenched in sweat. As soon as I want to stop, I will not be the best. Part of me begins to question if I can stop, but within a moment, the voice reminds me that if I stop, I will be fat because my body will have adjusted. Stopping equals weakness. The voice tells me I am not worthy of my Quest bar unless I am utterly exhausted.

On my way home from the last workout of the day, the voice drills in my mind a soundtrack of beliefs. The voice insists a minute more a day keeps the demons away. Every morning I must continue to check if I am small enough. The answer is always, "No! You are not. You must continue to do more."

Praises from the Gym

I am outside on the rec center patio in 80 degrees of humidity. With two Under Armour shirts, a gray sweatshirt, and thick leggings, I exhaust my body as I slam battle ropes on the concrete patio. Sweat drips down my face, as power radiates from my arms. My sweaty clothes get increasingly heavy. I set the timer for twenty minutes, and I won't stop until it rings. The energy moves to my toes, then up to my legs, through my core, and through my arms as I lift up the ropes and slam them onto the concrete. I perform this battle rope circuit with no water. I am only allowed to break for water after I complete at least two hours of cardio.

"You're an animal," the other gym rats tell me when they walk by, in awe.

"You have the best work ethic," the fitness junkies praise.

I soak in their compliments.

Every time I want to give up, I push on. Each time I begin to stop or pause, I hear one of these compliments repeating in my mind like a mantra. I have an identity in the gym that I need to uphold. If I stop, I'll no longer be the animal, fighting strong and proud. Each time I want to pause, the praise from other gym members keeps me burning.

"You're insane!" they tell me. Another compliment.

Maybe they're right. Maybe I'm out of my mind, but at least I no longer have a Santa Claus belly.

Destination Emptiness

Silence. Static, radio silence. I sit in my dad's ottoman chair after four hours of exhausting every ounce of my body. Big open windows frame the walls. The summer sunlight permeates through the glass. Pizza aromas fill the air. A Quest bar wrapper sits on the coffee table next to me. "Chasing Cars" plays softly in the background. With pride, I'm wearing XXS pink Nike shorts and an XS sports bra. My mom walks into the family room from her bedroom and glances over at me.

"Alz, what are you doing?"

I don't register the words coming from her mouth. I'm not aware of any words at all.

She asks again, louder, "Alz, did you hear me? What are you doing?"

I'm shocked by her harsh tone and look up. "Huh?" Her words confuse me. Why is she interrupting my TV time?

"I asked what you were doing."

"I'm watching TV."

"Alz, there's nothing on the TV. How are you watching it?"

I look up confused. I'm sure I'm watching TV, but the screen is completely black.

"Alz, I'm worried about you. Are you okay? You know you really need to fuel your body if you're going to be working out as long as you do. I thought we agreed you would try to shorten your workouts."

I nod. "Mom, I'm fine. Don't worry about me."

She walks off, avoiding another argument. I stare off into the blank screen. Staring at blank screens has become part of my daily routine.

I have longed for this silence. My mind is so consumed by racing and persistent thoughts that I long for this radio silence. The daily soundtrack starts from the moment I wake up. ED speaks to me on repeat.

You're not good enough.

Why haven't you worked out yet?

You're fat and disgusting.

Someone else is working harder than you right now.

You won't be the best just sitting there.

The soundtrack gets softer and softer the more I exhaust my body. Silence is my ultimate reward. I have worked away any thoughts I could possibly think. I have accomplished my goal for today. Eat less, move more, empty my thoughts, empty my soul. Become numb. Repeat.

Numbness is like the radio silence that fills the blank screen. It's like static energy that moves, but I cannot feel the movement. Only numbness.

Dreams once consumed my mind. With ED, blank screens, blank thoughts, and utter blankness consume my mind. So much blankness that I cannot hold a conversation with myself or with anyone else anymore. So much blankness that I don't know there's no noise coming from a TV that I presume is on. If I do not have to think or feel anymore, then I can just exist. I do not know emptiness is not the same as peace. Emptiness is a loss of self. Emptiness is an escape. The screen—blank. My mind—blank. My soul—blank.

Pain of Taste

I am boarding a flight to Europe with a group of high school students on a twelve-day study abroad trip. When I say goodbye to my parents, my dad assures me Europe will be good for me. He assumes I will go to Europe, eat some other food besides Quest bars and sweet potatoes, and come back healed. I know that isn't true.

I pack my TRX and my tennis shoes. I am determined that somehow, I'll find a way to exercise. I will eat as little as I can. I can't lose all the progress I've made. My parents hope this trip will serve me well. Yet the only place I want to be is at the rec center, clocking the hours away on the stair stepper. My parents have already paid for the trip, so I have no chance of backing out. My mom gives me a big hug, holding on tightly as I feel the anxiousness in her shaking arms. She is not as sure about this trip as my dad is.

My mom gives me my late Aunt Jane's angel wing engraved stone. She reminds me of the guardian angel that watches over me. She tells me that if I'm ever nervous, I can rub that stone and think of her and Aunt Jane. As we take off, I rub the stone whenever I stare at menus blankly, whenever the group is adventuring, and whenever I am consumed by thoughts of returning to the rec center.

The first few days, I remain on my plan, and I eat minimally. I struggle to find places to exercise, but I work in body weight circuits in the extremely small hotel corridors. As the days continue, my hunger increases.

On day four of twelve, we walk across Spain, taking in sights, sounds, and so much delicious-looking food. I decide to stray from my plan as I take a bite of a churro. As soon as I take a bite, it's like eating pop rocks. The sweet flavors sizzle in my mouth. The next day I try gelato, and every taste bud on my tongue lights up. LoLo, my best friend, tells me she is proud of me and excited to see me eating and trying new things.

With every pastry or taste of tapas, I tell myself to try what my dad wanted me to do—enjoy myself in my new environment. This freedom turns into an all-consuming consumption of every food in sight. My body welcomes each bite at first; it's been deprived for so long. But as I continue to eat from place to place and with my greatly reduced exercise regime, something else occurs in my body.

I wake up with swollen legs. I'm unable to bend my knees. I feel tingly all over, with a sensation of prickly pins and needles in my legs. As the day continues, walking becomes painful. By the fifth day, I can barely walk at all.

Back at our hotel room, I use the few minutes I have to call my parents and tell them about my pain. Walking up steps hurts; I can barely bend my knees. My parents talk to Senora Podway. She assures them it's likely just bad jet lag with all the traveling we've been doing.

My parents want to send me to the hospital in Spain or fly out themselves. They look at flights; I assure them I will be okay. I cannot convince myself of this. My parents tell me that when I'm back, we will go to the doctor and do a routine checkup. To appease them, I agree. However, I am already planning how to avoid seeing a doctor when I'm home. I now regret telling my parents about this pain. They will try to force me to get help, which I don't want.

I eat on our dinner boat cruise and instantly puke up every bite of food as the swelling becomes unbearable. Later I find out the pain I am experiencing is not jet lag. Instead, it's diagnosed as "refeeding syndrome."

Experiencing refeeding syndrome means my body is finally receiving nutrients it's been craving for a long time. But my body has been so deprived, it no longer knows what to do with this increase in food.

Instead of welcoming the nourishment, my body went into shock, which could have easily caused my heart to fail. I should have died.

I don't know what the Higher Power above is named. I do know there is someone named Jane, kept in a stone between my anxious palms, who carries me through.

Anorexic (I Am Not)

We get off the plane from Europe at Cleveland Hopkins International Airport after an eight-hour trip back. As I step off the plane, I have only one thing on my mind. I must get back to the Westlake Rec Center. I must go back to eating a Quest bar and a sweet potato only. I am convinced I have gained the weight of the world in the past two weeks. It's now time to get back to my "healthy routine." We collect our bags, and I begin to map out in my head how long it will take to get home and what time I can get to the rec center. However, my parents have a different plan.

I first see my mom. She runs fast to wrap me in her arms as my dad soon joins us; he wraps his arms around both my mom and me. All plans rush out of my head as I feel my parents' embrace. My tears flow fast and hard, like the water in a lake after winter is finally over. My body shakes, the tightness in my chest increases, and my breath catches in my throat. My mom holds me tighter; I feel a wet spot on my shoulder. My dad is stoic. Typically, you can hear his laughter whenever he enters a room. Today he is silent.

The Hirshes hug LoLo as LoLo looks over her shoulder at my family and me. She knows. I do not. All around us, other families are welcoming their kids home, some with tears, but that's different from what's happening with me and my parents. When they sent me off to Europe two weeks earlier, our goodbyes felt full of fear. Now, wrapped in their arms, I feel a desperate relief.

Even the words sound different today. Before I left, my dad told me, "You will be okay, buddy. Just try to eat the food and enjoy yourself."

Now, at the airport, he says, "We need to get you home. We can't keep doing this."

I remember our phone call and my promise to see a doctor. But I'd only agreed so they wouldn't send me to a hospital in Europe. The moment I said yes, I began strategizing how I'd convince them I didn't need to go. I'd say Europe helped me. I'd tell them I would eat some more food this time. Instead of going to the gym for four hours, I'd say I was going to the Metroparks or to a friend's house for part of the time, although the gym would actually be the only place I would go. I'd puke up my food if I was asked to eat more. Then I'd hide my scales, so they wouldn't find them.

As soon as we get home, I run upstairs to change into my sweatsuit, relieved I will be able to finally work out all the toxins I put in my body the past two weeks. I walk downstairs, and my mom grabs my hand.

"What are you doing?" I ask. "Let go. I'm going to the gym," I tell her.

"No, Alzie, you're not. We need to get you looked at. What happened in Europe was not okay. Remember, we talked about this on the phone, and you promised you'd go see a doctor when you got home."

"But Mom, I'm fine. I'm so much better now. Europe helped. I ate more food there. I'll do that here. I promise." I launch into my counterattack—all that strategizing I worked through to convince them I'm all right. But before I can continue, I look at my dad standing next to my mom, strong and firm. His seriousness is intimidating; my heart races as I don't know how to deal with this serious version of my dad.

"Buddy, you don't have a choice. You're getting in the car, and we're going to the doctor's now."

I let out screams and cries, no solid words, only a pure wail of desperation.

"I'm fine. I swear. I am fine." My pleas are fierce, hysteric, yet it doesn't shake my parents. My mom fights back tears as my dad firmly guides me to the car.

"You all are ruining my life. I'm fine. I don't need to go."

They give no response. There is no point in arguing with a human who is consumed by a devil within. The entire car ride, I don't speak. I fume with rage and disgust. I'm ready to boil over like a pot of water whose temperature is now too high because the lid has been kept on too long. I need to escape. Staring out the window, I try to create my Plan B. As we pull into the parking lot, I realize I've run out of ideas.

Most seventeen-year-olds go into the doctor's office alone. However, for this visit, both my parents come in with me. I imagine they're afraid I will run if they don't accompany me. The nurse calls my name. I step onto the scale. Looking down, I study the number: 120 pounds—four pounds too heavy and ten pounds away from my goal weight. In my mind, if I am five feet, eight inches, and the "average" weight range is around 140 pounds, then I must be at least thirty pounds lighter or more. I will not be average. Seeing the scale, I know I must get to the gym after this appointment. I wonder how I can get there.

The nurse takes my heart rate, but she doesn't share the results. Instead, she asks us to please stay here and states Dr. Greenberg will be with us immediately. My body is filled with fear as I glance at my parents exchanging nervous stares.

Dr. Greenberg asks me a string of fuzzy questions about how I've been feeling, if I think I may be working out too much, and what I typically eat in a day. I lie and tell her I eat more than I normally do, and that after Europe, I now will eat more. I lie and tell her I only spend about two hours at the gym.

My dad begins to correct me. My mom pulls him back and gently whispers to "let it be." Dr. Greenberg asks my parents to step outside for a moment as I sit anxiously alone among four white walls. I don't know what they're saying behind that door.

Dr. Greenberg is a calm, collected, patient, and empathetic doctor. She has watched me grow from a tiny human to this seventeen-year-old young woman. However, she doesn't know who this person is in front of her. The once smiley and energetic girl is now sitting on her table—angry, anxious, and desperately thin.

As they reenter the room, my parents can't bear to look at me. Dr. Greenberg sits close to me and gently places her hand on my knee.

"Allyson, have you ever heard of anorexia?"

No. No. No. This can't be happening. My mom attempts to appear strong as she tries not to cry. My dad looks at the ground, emotionless. My throat catches as a mix of tears, screams, and pure panic fills my entire body. I try to answer her without sobbing.

"I've heard of it, but I don't have it. That's not me."

"Well, honey, I think it is. You are anorexic."

No. No. No. I have no control over my tears this time. My entire body shakes as I hold my wet face in my palms.

"That can't be true. I'm just very healthy. That can't be possible. People who are anorexic don't eat. I eat! So that can't be right. You have no idea what you're talking about."

My parents say nothing. Dr. Greenberg attempts to calm me down.

"Allyson, I know you eat, but you are very sick, and we need to get you help. I believe you need to go to the hospital. I don't know how long, but we can't help you fully here."

I stare at my parents.

"Did you know about this? Why are you letting them do this? I don't need to go to the hospital. I just need to eat a little more and work out a little less. I'm fine. I eat. I'll be fine. Sick people go to the hospital. I don't need to go. I'm not sick."

My mom finally talks. "Honey, it will be okay. I know this is a lot, but we need to get you some help. You want to keep living this life, right?"

She is wrong. I don't want to keep living if living does not mean abundant exercise and Quest bars. I don't confirm her assumption. Instead, I stare petrified, as my dad stands, takes my hand, and gently kisses my forehead.

"It's okay, buddy. We will get through this." I don't hug or kiss him back. He is part of the plan to ruin my life and ruin me. Then he turns to Dr. Greenberg and asks her what the next steps are. I have no say.

"I will call the Cleveland Clinic now and see how soon we can get her in. Realistically, we could take an ambulance from here now."

"NO!" I finally make my voice heard. "I'm not going now."

My mom's empathy forces her to step in. "Let's go home and at least let your sister know. We can get things together and then go from there. Please call us when you have more information."

My dad firmly guides me to the car again. The silence is even louder on the way home. No music drowns out the quiet. In the rearview mirror I can see my parents exchanging nervous glances, while I create Plan C. I must escape. I have twenty-four hours. I can't live this new reality.

I sprint upstairs as soon as we get home, slamming the door with rage. This can't be happening. I begin to pack a bag to run away, any way to escape this hell. I determine that LoLo, my best friend, will believe me. She'll also think they're all crazy. So I text her to inform her of this new reality, assuming she'll see the truth and help me escape.

But she doesn't. She tells me she also thinks I need to go to the hospital, that she's worried about me, that she can't help me either, that she wants me to live, and that she loves me. How can my best friend love me if she is on their team? How can my best friend want me to get better if she thinks I need to go to the hospital?

I'm convinced they're all in a mutual plan to strip me of any health I have; that they don't know what health means; that they are jealous of how healthy I have become; that they're wanting to find any opportunity to control me; that they know absolutely nothing.

My dad calls me from my room to come to our downstairs living room. My mom still cannot meet my eyes.

"Tomorrow morning we're going to go to the Cleveland Clinic," my dad says.

"I fucking hate you both. You are ruining my life!" I scream.

I don't sleep that night. I'm unable to fathom that even though I'm the healthiest person I know, I'm going to the hospital. Sick people go to the hospital. I'm not sick. They don't know anything. I alone know the truth.

A Week Left to Live

I lie in the hospital bed, finally achieving my version of a finish line—
ultimate thinness—at seventeen years old. I crossed it, with one week
left to live. My prize is a green-and-yellow-checkered hospital gown and
sticky white pads on my chest. The sticky white pads track my exhausted
heart. The rhythm of the machine next to me tracks the slow ebbs and
flows of the mere twenty-six beeps that pass every minute.

My breath is shallow; the bare walls close in on me. I don't know
how many morsels of food I am forced to consume, or what time of day
it is, or how long I've been lying here, or how I can escape. Silence pene-
trates the emptiness. The only indication of time is the red light flashing
next to my bed and the hourly vital checks by blurry figures in scrubs.
They hold my fragile bones to check the beeping of my weakened heart.

Figures donned in white lab coats drift in and out of the room. Noise
flows from their mouths, yet only one phrase registers in my brain.

"One week left to live."

PART 3

Fighting On

On July 24, 2013, four white walls watch a girl in a checkered gown. Her breath is slow and shallow. She lies there, nearly lifeless. Like a newborn baby, she spends most of her days sleeping and being awakened to eat. Like a newborn baby, the only things she needs are nutrients and rest.

Trays pass in and out of the room, always accompanied by her tears. Her mood completely shifts as soon as a tray appears in her view; her hands begin to shake; her breath turns from shallow bellows to fast-paced wheezing. She can't catch a full breath either way.

Another older woman stays in the room with her often. This older woman looks at the girl with compassion in her eyes. Each time the woman looks at her, the girl's stone blue eyes become glassy with desperation. She tells the girl she can "do this" and squeezes her hand gently when the young girl doubts herself.

Different women in purple and blue scrubs lift her frail body up from time to time. She cannot lift herself up. They wrap a blue cuff around her arm every three hours and ask her to sit still for thirty seconds at a time, lying, then sitting, and finally standing. She moves very slowly between these positions with a good deal of assistance from the women in scrubs. She is hooked up to a machine at all times to track some type of metric to ensure her life carries on. This monitor beeps next to her and consistently goes off every few minutes; it beeps when the metric falls below 40 BPM. The women in scrubs also roll over a small white, bucket-like apparatus the girl uses as a bathroom. She never leaves the room or goes to a bathroom that isn't by her bed.

Some of the women in scrubs are kind and encourage her, hold her hand if she allows it, and give her extra time to finish the trays when she asks. Others use a more forceful method and start the clock the moment the tray is opened, stating bluntly that she won't live if she doesn't eat.

A man is often there, trying to add humor to every situation, yet typically he is silent. He nervously paces around the room. This, too, makes the girl nervous as she asks him often, "Dad, please sit down." A young woman also comes and lies on the couch or holds the girl's hand. She is also often silent.

A very important-looking woman comes in one time each day and often provides news that makes the young girl angry. This woman is wearing a white coat and usually tells her she is not able to escape these four white walls yet, that she must continue to lie motionless and eat to bolster her heart. The young girl looks more hopeless and depleted each time that white coat leaves.

A dry erase board documents her everyday state. A smile rating is used to track her pain for the day, numbers that account for her heart rate and other vitals, and a time chart to track the food she will be consuming that day. What is wrong with her? Why is she supervised all the time? Why is she woken up every few hours to get something put on her arm? Is she even really alive?

Slowly her smiles become slightly more frequent; the heart rate monitor beeps a little less. For the first time in four days, she is allowed to leave. Instead of being lifted up to have the blue cuff wrapped around her arm, she is lifted up to sit in a wheelchair. It's her first time unhooked from the machine.

Swimming in Circles

The third-floor halls are suffocating, white, and bare. The only decoration consists of a giant fish tank that my dad chooses as the destination of my daily wheelchair rides. My fear of not fitting through doors became true, not because of weight gain, but from the four-wheeled chair I use for these thirty-minute daily rides.

I lie nearly lifeless in bed. My dad paces back and forth. His nervous energy permeates the room. He does not do well with emotion. He only knows how to add humor or run from emotional situations, especially ones that are as barren as the walls around us.

"Wanna go for a ride, buddy?"

I glance up at him and gently nod my head. Yes, I will go wherever he wheels me.

As my dad wheels the wheelchair next to the bed, the 24/7 Russian nurse grabs one of my arms to help me. I slowly sit up because moving too fast will cause my head to spin, see stars, and potentially pass out.

I take a few steps to get into the wheelchair. Part of me wants to turn those two steps into a full-blown run out of these four white walls, yet another part of me does not want to move at all, as I can feel my heart beating so slowly, and my legs are still swollen from edema.

My dad awkwardly smiles and makes some kind of joke like he always does. I don't know what he says, but the nurse laughs, and I stare off into the abyss of the white walls.

"Okay, let's go! This will be fun!"

My dad starts our route: to the right, down the hall, stopping to say hi and making another joke to the receptionists. The nurse comes with us because I am not allowed to be without medical supervision. She walks a few steps behind. Maybe she thinks this will give my dad and me some one-on-one time to connect.

My dad's idea of bonding is going to the fish tank. Perhaps he thinks staring at fish will remind me of my childhood and the fish tank we had in our basement growing up.

"Buddy, look at the fish. They're pretty cool, right?"

"Sure, Dad," I say. Mustering any other words will require energy I don't have. We sit in front of the fish tank staring, saying nothing. Perhaps he thinks looking at fish will make his daughter "normal" again. Normal. I don't even know what that means.

This tank full of fish provides the only color in the hall—a vision of crystal blue water and the bright, vibrant hues of the confined fish. I try to breathe in deeply to register this moment, but all I can do is stare blankly at the glass. The fish understand me. They swim in circles, lacking an expansive ocean. They swim fast, perhaps trying to escape. They swim into the glass walls, definitely trying to escape. But there is no escape. There are only thirty-minute wheelchair rides to stare at the fish as they stare back at me.

Begin Again

On the fifth day, my sister takes me on a wheelchair ride. We head over to the gift shop. She is soft-spoken and quiet, unsure of what to say, since she's not used to seeing her sister unable to walk. She wheels me up and down the small aisles of the gift store, stopping at the journal section.

She pulls out an orange journal with "I AM DOING MY BEST" in a big, bold white font on the front cover. Each page of the journal has a quote on the left-hand side and a place to write on the right-hand side, with a question about how I am doing indicated by the image of a glass. For each entry, you can choose a full glass, a half-full glass, a glass where the liquid spills over, or a glass completely empty.

"Hey, Al. What if you get this journal? You can use it to write as you lie in bed and after meals. You used to love writing! Maybe this will help."

I nod a silent yes as my brain still struggles to process all that is happening around me. We buy the journal. I begin to write to heal my mind, process all that is happening inside of me, and begin again.

Journal Entry, July 28, 2013

"I have an eating disorder. It's scary to hear those words come from my mouth, but it's the truth. Previously I used to not believe someone could be anorexic or bulimic, being ignorant, and not thinking anything of it because I had not walked in their shoes.

Though now I know ED is no joking matter. He is controlling, evil, and corrupt. Every second, every minute, twenty-four hours, seven days a week, my mind is consumed by these thoughts. Consumed on every fixated calorie and nutrition fact, the guilt of eating one simple cookie or having an undocumented handful of trail mix.

The necessity to get the "poison" out of my body and after eating, the obsession of checking my stomach after every meal and periodically throughout the day to see if it had gotten fat. Working out for hours on end, jumping from machine to machine, making myself look like "Superwoman" from the outside as I tried to complete each task, though feeling torn, beaten, and exhausted inside. My foot hurt. "Suck it up and run," ED screamed. I was tired and could probably benefit from a rest day. "Don't you dare rest, or you'll get fat," belittled ED. The constant battle of thoughts in my mind depleted all sense of pleasure and happiness I once had. Before meals, ED made me do a quick set of push-ups, so I would not get fat from the meal I would soon be eating.

While my mind is still consumed by ED, I know it will get better one step at a time. It won't be easy; it's fighting hell. I'm ready to have a life, along with a lifestyle, of healthy food and work-outs, not a life taken over by obsession with healthy foods and workouts."

Journal Entry, July 29, 2013

"Today is the start of a new journey, where my mind is no longer corrupted by ED.

List of new goals:

- Eat froyo with friends with no guilt or feeling of the need to vomit.

- Go out to eat with family and not research nutritional content and choose whichever meal looks good.
- Make lunch/dinner with my mom without measuring or getting super anxious about the caloric intake.
- Still want to maintain a healthy lifestyle but in a balanced/controlled manner.

List of questions for the doctors:

- Will Mom know the amount to give and how many nutrients I need at meals?
- Are you giving my mom meal ideas, or does she come up with them on her own?
- Are Quest bars still okay to eat?

My Brain on a Brownie

I finish a tray of food in front of me: a turkey sandwich, some secret power shake that is likely packed with copious amounts of hidden fat, an apple, and some other food I don't fully register. I take a deep breath and ask the nurse if I can have my paints.

After each meal, I paint to steady and calm my mind and my hands. I keep the brush between my fingers and grab a wooden letter. I think of them as "Letters of Life." Truly, they are the only thing that helps me hang onto this painful life my body currently exists in. I use shades of blue as I paint repetitive small lines and circles that exist on their own, yet flow into one another, creating blends of colors and shapes. After each meal, I paint to escape the thoughts of wanting to empty myself of all the "poison" I just put in my body.

The nurse looks at me with a look of pity and sorrow, combined with some degree of compassion. I wonder why she has not brought me my paints yet. She tells me I can't paint yet. I look at her, confused. Maybe the child life specialist who usually brings the painting supplies isn't here today. Maybe someone else is using the paints today. But what she says next, I cannot comprehend. "You have one more thing to eat before you can paint today."

There are some rules in the hospital that must be followed:

- I will be given meals and snacks I must eat and cannot choose.
- A nutritionist will plan my meals, despite the exhaustive list of items I tell her I do not like (essentially everything except Quest bars, carrots, and sweet potatoes).

- I am not allowed to eat any food that is brought in from the outside world.
- I will be watched the entire time during my meals and snacks, so I can't hide any food.
- I have forty-five minutes to finish my plate.
- After I finish my plate, I cannot use the restroom for a minimum of one hour.
- When I am strong enough to walk, I can use the restroom, but only with the door open.
- After I use the restroom, I cannot flush because the people in charge must check that I didn't puke up my meal.

My body feels so hot and sweaty, like I just sat outside for a solid thirty minutes in the humid summer heat. I can't stop my brain from spiraling.

"But I just finished my food. I did what you told me. I cleaned my plate. It's not time for my snack yet."

"I know, but you are strong, and I know you can do this. We think you're ready to try this challenge," she says calmly.

I do not want to be challenged. I want to calm my mind. I want to steady my shaking hands and hold my paintbrush.

Another nurse comes in holding a white plate with another plate on top, hiding what is underneath. I want to scream and punch something: a pillow, a person, anything. I don't even know yet what awaits me, but I assume it's not good.

The nurse raises my bed up, and I look at my mom with dread. Her eyes look at mine and then slightly away, as if to say, "I'm sorry for what is coming, but I love you." The nurse places the plate in front of me and slowly opens the top. At this point, I want to rip the top off to know what disgusting food I am going to be forced to put in my body. And then I see it.

A brownie. A fucking brownie. Nooooooo! A brownie is on the forbidden list. I did not authorize anyone to give me a brownie. Is this some kind of sick joke? Do they actually believe I will eat this gross, poisonous, brown toxin?

The four walls begin to collapse around me. I can't do this. This must be the end.

If I eat this brownie, it will be the end. I cry, then sob, and then shriek. Within five minutes of seeing the brownie, I'm convinced I will be dead if I'm forced to eat this.

I can hardly think as my overloaded body is just trying to find its next breath. But I do know:

- This brownie is filled with sugar, processed ingredients, and everything bad in this world.
- This brownie will immediately make me gain fifty pounds or more.
- This brownie will instantly deprive me of all my self-control.

My mom looks at me, though I can't meet her gaze as my tears fall onto the fudgy, chocolatey, and now soggy brownie.

"You can do this," the nurse says.

I look over at Mom. I see the guilt in her eyes as she gave them approval to serve me this brownie.

"Can she at least have more than forty-five minutes for this one?" she asks.

"We can give her an hour," the nurse says, "but if she won't eat it, then she will need the tube."

The tears flow faster as my chest contracts.

My mom crawls into the twin-size hospital bed and cradles my body. She grabs my hands and rubs them slowly between her palms. She holds her seventeen-year-old daughter, steadying me as my breath slows down to match the rhythm of hers.

I don't know how I will eat this brownie. I do know it will be better than a tube. Once my breath has relaxed, my mom takes the fork and gently places it in my hand as she wraps hers around mine. With her help, I finish the brownie, one small bite at a time.

Rooftop with a View

I sit on the Cleveland Clinic rooftop on the seventeenth floor, my mom by my side. Car horns, train engines, and the city breeze flood my eardrums. Fresh air fills my lungs. I can finally breathe. For forty-five minutes, I can pretend my reality is not what it is on the third floor. I can imagine I am well and healthy. I can visualize myself on a summer rooftop with the breeze blowing in my long brown hair. But looking down at my chair and gown, I am reminded of the actuality of my world.

The hospital gown drapes over my bones. The summer air is sticky and hot, yet I shiver as my weak heart attempts to pump fresh blood through my veins. Physically I am finally on top, sitting on this roof instead of languishing on the third floor. Now that I'm here, I can look out at the entire world that has been there for the past seventeen years of my life. Time freezes. My mind stills. My mother's hand gently touches my shoulder, and she whispers, as a wet drop falls upon my skin, "How did we get here?"

Below the vast cotton candy skyline, I feel so small. My mom's hand rests on my shoulder. She is unusually quiet. We both are. I am flooded with emotion, like waking up from a bad dream that seems so real you're unsure if it's true. This isn't a dream. I begin to understand the gravity of life and how much power my mind has had over me.

If this were that dream, I'd be falling, falling so fast that I can't stop myself from falling, and at the very moment I think I'm going to crash, somehow something catches me. In my physical bed, I often feel myself sinking deeper into the mattress, but then, at the very last second when something catches me in the dream, my body is jolted awake, and I wake up. Then I feel confused and shaken but a bit relieved it was just a dream after all.

Nearing death is somewhat like that. ED's voice is way too loud, and then somehow, someway, someone steps in and catches me, grabs my hand, and tells me this doesn't need to be my reality. If I fall, I don't have to crash.

Journal Entry, July 31, 2013 (from the rooftop)

"The simplicity of a smile is truly taken for granted. It has been so long since the precious sound of laughter has let loose from my soul. My soul is now free. Here, I look at life with more respect and gratitude than words can describe. My mother's precious hand rests upon my back as I get stronger every second, step by step. I gaze into the beautiful sunset and smile the simplest smile. Looking at life with different eyes, life is a beautiful thing. Life truly is good."

Sister TLC

Most of our lives, I took up the space as my sister quietly meandered through the world. Yet here we are among these four walls, and I am now the silent one. My sister doesn't use this as an opportunity to switch places. Instead, she is equally quiet. She takes a back seat to my dad's anxious pacing and my mom's all-consuming care. She holds my hand, and I can feel her love through her touch.

We don't ask each other how we are. Siblings don't need words. Four years older and a soon-to-be college senior, Lauren endures her own battles. Here I am again, trying to take away the spotlight.

I don't fault my sister for staying silent. She finds other ways to show me she cares. We spend nights once I'm home driving the streets of the Cleveland suburbs blasting "Hey, Soul Sister" and singing at the top of our lungs. She shows me she cares through mockery and silliness. She often doesn't know what to say at the moment, so she doesn't say anything at all. Instead, she shows her support through written letters slipped underneath my pillow after coming home from the clinic.

Al,

I love you, and I just want to see you happy, so please read this. If you get upset one day, try using this; it may help. You can also think it's stupid, and I'm just a hippie freak. But please just take the time to read this.

Celebrate every success. Be happy for completing a project no matter the grade because you are smart enough to complete it. Celebrate living, breathing, walking every day because you are luckier than most. Find your passion. Love the life you are living.

Your passion may not be apparent for years, but when you realize it, never let anything stop you.

Now that's a big dose of advice, so here's what I want you to do first. First ask yourself every morning:

1. *What's going to be today's adventure?*
2. *Who am I going to help today?*

Ask yourself those questions, and you will see life in a different way. Second, make a chart where one side is stressors and one side is reliefs. Stressors are things that make you upset, and reliefs are things that make you happy. This can't include working out because that's already part of your daily routine. Now every day, when you let something stress you out on the list, put an X, and when something doesn't stress you out on the list, put a checkmark. For every stressor, you must complete as many reliefs. I dare you to try to see the results. Life is meant to be lived, so go live!

She sees the best of me and my future. My sister is my strength, and through our silence, I find solace.

My Recovery Math Problems

My recovery math problems are compiled of simple if-then statements. If I complete certain tasks, then I am recovered. If I eat my food and gain weight, then I am recovered. If I eat out at restaurants, then I am recovered. If I go to school and get an A+ on everything, showing my brain is working, then I am recovered.

And yet, I wake up, and I feel anything but recovered. Instead, I am filled with anxiety and frustration. My hands shake at the mere thought of eating food. The mirror tells me that if I continue to gain weight, then I will be a worthless piece of shit. I journal out the pain inside my mind.

"Screw all of this. I am done. This food is empty calories. It's not good for me. Ugh I'm DONE!"

A few days later, there is hope. I check a few more accomplishments off my recovery list, including helping to cook my own meals and grocery shopping.

"I feel like I am really progressing. I was able to prepare dinner with my mom and put my own salad dressing on without measuring it. At the store, I put two of my old favorite foods in the cart that I used to restrict."

The hope only lasts a short while, as the thoughts begin to torment me again.

"I just want to run away forever. Fuck this. Fuck this. Fuck this. I'm DONE!"

I'm convinced recovery is just like calculating my calorie intake in MyFitnessPal. I try to calculate the exact equation that will accomplish this "recovery state." Yet, there is no equation to recovery. There is only living in the gray, in the extreme highs and extreme lows, the pain and joy. There are only attempts to continue to carry on and get back up again and again.

CCED

Her red, bouncy hair mimics her fiery energy as she skips over to me, suspiciously energetic for being in a rehab program. She hugs me as if I am a long-lost friend.

"Hi! I'm Annie! I'm so glad you're here. You'll love it here. We are all so supportive, and you're going to be so strong by the end of this! Do you like art? We have art every day. It's my favorite part of being here."

What kind of crazy meds are they giving these kids? How old is this girl? She can't be older than thirteen. Poor girl. I can't imagine being so young. I pause, as I realize I haven't said anything, and I'm just standing, still judging and staring at this stranger in front of me.

"Uh, hi, I'm Allyson, nice to meet you."

I usually am the bubbly and receptive kind. But today I want to be anywhere but here. CCED is the Cleveland Center for Eating Disorders. The doctors demand I go to CCED to continue the recovery process.

I am supposed to be starting my senior year with my friends. I am not supposed to be surrounded by annoyingly energetic twelve-year-olds. I already did my recovery period in the hospital. I am cured now. I ate a brownie in the hospital. Now I should go back to my daily work-outs and tell my story to help others.

The first day at CCED, we meet Dr. Blake. He's a bald white man who listens to me and nods his head while simultaneously making me feel inferior. He starts to explain a concept called Maudsley to my parents, not once looking at me, as if this conversation isn't even about me. Essentially, the Maudsley plan is supposed to help restore my weight to normal levels given my age and height. Then they hand the control over my eating back to me and encourage age-appropriate development.

While I hear Dr. Blake say that this approach has proven benefits and is successful for many people, I'm positive it will not be successful for me. I do not want anyone else to be in control of my plan. I know what's right for me, not my parents.

As he explains Maudsley to my parents, I sit like a ghost in the background.

"Are you sure this will work?" my dad asks.

My mom shushes him and tells him to trust the experts as she feverishly writes down notes while the doctor continues to explain the Maudsley plan. My dad looks at me, empathy in his eyes. My parents leave with a binder, a workbook, my dad's pure skepticism, and my mom's plethora of notes. I return to the group.

I stare at the girls around me during our first meal together. I am eating everything the treatment team puts in my mystery brown bag. The reward for weight restoration is I can work out again, so I will do anything in my power to get back to working out, even if that means eating milkshakes and other disgusting food.

At the meal table, Annie's personality from this morning is nowhere to be found. Instead, she is crying because she can't bear to eat her turkey sandwich. A group counselor walks Katie, a tiny eleven-year-old, away from the table while whispers of "the tube" float around the table. Annie is told that if she can't finish within the allotted time, she will need to get her food "another way." We all know what this means. Another girl takes Annie's hand gently and gives her encouraging words: "You can do it. I believe in you." Annie takes one bite as tears pour down her face.

These girls are so much sicker than me. I don't belong here. They likely haven't even had their first kiss or know what an AP class is. I have classes to take, senior prom to plan, football games to go to, friends to see again, my story of resilience to tell. I am not supposed to be in a stupid rehab program.

I make my exit plan. I know my dad was suspicious from the start, so I start with him. If I can convince him I should leave, then I will be free of these dumb doctors and their stupid rehab place. My mom will be a bit harder to persuade. She will do anything, listen to anyone, just to get me back to "normal."

I tell them the other girls are much younger and sicker than I am. I say I learned a lot in the hospital, and if I can just get my weight restored, I will be able to work out in a healthy way again. I tell them staying in this program will be too triggering. I promise I will go to doctor appointments and eat the food they put in front of me. I tell them anything to convince them leaving CCED is better than staying.

My arguments work, and we withdraw from the program. The doctors disapprove, and the other girls are shocked I am leaving so early. They write me goodbye letters, complimenting me on my ability to get out of there so fast. We don't know this early exit is really getting further away from recovery. My parents are lost now. ED has outsmarted us all.

Will It Ever Get Better?

Journal Entry, August 14, 2013

"School. What will they think? Will they notice the newly gained fat on my face and thighs? Will they laugh? Will my mind allow me to let those thoughts fall away? I try to tell myself it doesn't matter what 'they' say. I try to stay strong, but sometimes it's so hard not to enjoy being a teenager. I regret putting myself in this position, and I know the doctors say it's not my fault, but I guess sometimes that bullshit is just way too hard to fathom. I want to get better, but this is just so damn frustrating."

Journal Entry, August 15, 2013

"It's not about tomorrow. It's about today. It's about smiles and laughter, not about society's idealistic principles of perfection and image. If you don't have family and friends around you to support and love you, then you really have nothing. I know I'll have my ups and downs, but I'm not backing down. I want to laugh so hard it hurts. That's what I want more than any specific body shape."

Journal Entry, August 24, 2013

"I'm so annoyed today and DO NOT want to eat. My mom is so frustrating! I hate when she gives me choices or contemplates foods in front of me. I feel like she's trying to make me recover faster than I can. I don't want to eat, and she doesn't get it! I'm not okay, and no one understands."

Journal Entry, August 25, 2013

"Food is getting harder and harder to eat. I wish I could have a normal relationship with food. I'm scared I'll never be able to do that and that I'll never be okay."

Journal Entry, September 2, 2013

"Some days I'd rather be thin than healthy. The flat stomach, the toned body, the hardship of eating. Some days I'm so scared of never recovering."

Journal Entry, September 3, 2013

"I feel so ugly and fat, and I've never felt so uncomfortable going into a school year. I used to be so skinny and pretty, and I want that back. I'm so done. Congrats, ED, you have won. I give up. Why would a fat piece of shit like me even want to live?"

Journal Entry, September 26, 2013

"This fucking sucks. I hate life. I can't believe my heart rate is at 47. This is awful. I hate life. My birthday is Wednesday, and this is the worst present I could ever receive. I just want to give up. I'm done fighting. I just don't want to live at all anymore. I hate myself."

Somehow, like the brief, intense light of a sparkler on a dark summer night, I hold onto the hope I will someday be okay.

Moving Again

Journal Entry, September 1, 2013

"New month, new attitude. I will remain positive and look to God when I'm anxious or angry. I will trust my mom and know she is feeding me properly. I'm excited to form a healthy relationship with working out soon and no longer view it as punishment. Some days, I feel I won't survive. I feel no one understands, and they all think I am fine now. Now it's harder than ever. I need to stay strong."

Journal Entry, September 5, 2013

"Today was absolutely incredible! My vitals were great! I have workout privileges again and can go back to work one day a week. I went on a run for the first time. It felt so great! I know this is the hardest part, but I can beat ED one step at a time!"

Journal Entry, September 16, 2013

"I'm kind of nervous about my first real workout again, and I'm just scared ED will take over and force me to work out crazily like before."

Journal Entry, October 9, 2013

"I got my period! I'm so excited! I feel so normal! Training with Thad was incredible today! He let me push my limits, and it felt so great. I realized today that I am beautiful. I feel so lucky to have people like Thad, my sissy, and my parents to help me in times of need and support me. Life is wonderful."

Journal Entry, October 17, 2013

"Fuck this. The doctors are royal idiots. They're mad at me for being happy with my body and want me to hate myself again. They think they know it all, but they're merely idiots who only know facts. This has been the worst senior year I could have ever imagined. Mom's an idiot because she believes the doctors. All of my college apps are in, so school doesn't even matter any-more. I'm so ready to leave and get the hell out of here and as far away from doctors as possible. I'm not gaining weight, and I am fine now."

Journal Entry, October 28, 2013

"I've eaten so much, but I am hoping it will pay off for weigh-in. It sucks having to gain weight in a world where everyone is fixated on losing it. I just have to remind myself that health is so much more important than vanity. God doesn't care what I look like. He just wants me to love life. So, although I may not be at my 'ideal' body image, I am getting healthier, which is far more important. I'm healthy. I can work out without depleting my body, walk, hang with friends, and most importantly, I can live."

Journal Entry, October 31, 2013

"Ah! I went running today! I ran almost four miles in twenty-eight minutes! My mind was clear, and I just embraced nature and life. I felt God through my body as I was running. Although my body was getting tired, I began to think of who mattered and how it's not about me. I ran for my amazing parents, for Nana, and those who can't run. I feel confident about my body! I am proud of how far I have come! I couldn't do it without my loved ones by my side!"

I feel the tingling in my lungs the second I get a dose of moving again. The rapid beating of my heart reminds me how fully alive I am. I have felt so empty, detached, and lost for the past sixty days that even the smallest dose of movement creates fires in my brain. When I move again, it's hard to hold back. Like a Christmas tree, every node in my brain lights up, reigniting pathways that remember what it feels like to move: painful, exhausting, yet so fulfilling.

This time, I can't move until exhaustion. I see someone running, and I want to run again. I begin to move, and I want to keep moving endlessly. I feel alive, and I want to continue to feel this. Movement is the most immediate way I know to feel alive.

They tell me to be careful and not push too far. Thad, my trainer, suggests I take it one step at a time. My dad reminds me I don't want to be back where I was before. Yet moving again is so integral to who I am. It's my identity. I don't know how to move with ease, so I continue to push myself, thinking that I'm moving in a healthy way (because it's only two hours instead of four).

I coach young girls in my trainer's gym and see joy in their eyes when they move their bodies. I want to cultivate this childlike movement in my body, but the call to do more is too strong, so I continue to move forcefully. I tell myself I'm moving with ease so I can convince my parents I have it all under control. Yet ED tells me that in a few months, I'll get rid of anyone who is holding me back. So I carry on, hiding my movement, doing extra planks when no one is watching, pushing through any pain I may feel. I'm moving again. I'm alive. But I'm still not okay.

When Love is not Enough

Journal Entry, September 11, 2013

"I hate my eating disorder. No one understands. They all think I'm fine, but I'm not. I'm fat and ugly, and I don't want to eat. The thoughts are never-ending, and I take everything personally. My parents keep fighting, and my mom is so overwhelmed. I don't want her to feel this way. It would be so much easier if one of my runs would just give me a heart attack."

I close my journal and go for a run that I'm not supposed to go on. After the run, I begin to do core exercises out on our deck. My body is in a plank as my dad runs out, smoke coming from his ears. My body shakes from the strength of the plank and soon begins shaking in fear as I hear my dad scream.

"Allyson Rae! Why in the hell did you just run? You know you're not supposed to! We cannot keep dealing with this shit if you don't help yourself. Do you even want to live?"

His laughter is replaced by fury; I am not used to this version of him. He is the man who dresses up in a bunny suit from *A Christmas Story* to take pictures for our family holiday card. He is the man who wears backward caps and cutoff shirts at the gym at fifty years old and still calls people "bro." He is driven by humor, not anger.

Now my dad is beyond angry. I continue to hold the plank, my fore-arms quivering, my heart beating strong, as my iPhone timer counts down the forty-seven seconds remaining until I can respond to my dad's anger.

"Do you hear me? What is it going to take to get you to stop?"

Stop? Keep going.

Do not listen to him. He is trying to control you.

Keep going.

Ignore him long enough for him to realize he has no control over you.

Do not stop. Ever.

As I continue to ignore him, my dad walks back in the house, slam-ming the door. Thirty minutes later, after more core work and stretching, I walk back inside to complete silence. It's like I am a ghost to my par-ents. As I storm off, I am determined to not let their silent treatment win. They have no control. Only ED does, as he slowly slips his way back into owning my entire being.

I stay in my room until they call me down to eat dinner. It's the last thing I want to do. ED reminds me I have already won one battle today by ignoring my dad and pushing my body; it's now time to win again.

After a few bites, I put down my knife and fork.

"No, Allyson. You are *going* to eat. You did way too much today already. You must eat."

I don't look up at my dad. I don't pick up my fork. Silence permeates the entire space again, until my mom breaks it.

"Alz, we are just trying to help. We love you, and we want you to live. You need to fuel your body."

Like a warm, itchy blanket, her words touch my body with care, yet there is so much discomfort that I can't let that kindness in. I want to answer them. I want them to know I love them. But right now, I love ED more. Again, I say nothing. Instead, I run upstairs, cry vehemently, and begin to punch my pillow.

I hate them. I hate them so much. They are trying to ruin my life!

The anger continues to rage in my body, as the punches become faster and stronger, and the pillow doesn't react back. I'm overwhelmed by the need to break something. I want something to feel as broken as I feel inside. Somehow I decide it will be my towel rack. A newfound strength takes over my body as I rip the towel rack out of the wall, resulting in a resounding thud.

"What was that?"

I hear my mom racing up the stairs.

She finds me on the floor, tears streaming down my face. She wraps me in her arms to ease my shaking body. "Shh, Alzie, it's okay. I love you."

My dad comes upstairs to see what's happening. He tells me he loves me too. I can't understand why they love me, despite all I have done.

Again and Again and Again

"We're losing her."

Finn is in the room with me as everything begins to cave in. Finn is a caring young man whom I have come to know and care for during this time. He surprises me at the hospital with flowers and a hug. It feels normal to laugh again and connect with someone besides doctors and family.

My mom steps out of the room to let us have some time to connect; the nurse remains there with us. Finn and I talk as I show him my new paintings. Suddenly the walls blur together, and I feel my breath become shallow as pain floods across my chest. Finn realizes something is off and calls out for my mom. The 24/7 nurse rushes to my side, checking my vitals.

Mom races in. I can hear her screech, "Alz, Alz, what's going on? Alz, stay with us . . ."

She grabs my hand. I feel her touch, but I can't respond. I don't stay, despite her pleading, as my world goes dark. I hear glimpses of murmurs like faint voices in a distant world. And then everything goes black.

I wake up in the ICU where my mom tells me that if I'd been awake, this is what I would have seen and heard:

"She doesn't look like she has an eating disorder to me," says the doctor, who has never treated me before. "I'm not really sure what to do."

"She's sick," my mom insists. "Please help her, please!"

The nurses talk to me, getting me on oxygen, trying all they can to keep me alive. Despite being on oxygen, I am continuously losing oxygen.

Too much time passes, and they rush me to the ICU where I wake up eight hours later.

When I wake up, I have no idea what happened. My mom is allowed to stay with me in the ICU, even though that's against hospital protocol. Later my mom tells me that during those eight hours, she sat on the chair next to me, praying I would wake up soon. As soon as my eyes opened, my mom jumped up from the chair, grabbed my hand, and gave me the gentlest kiss on my forehead.

"I am so happy you are okay."

I looked at her, then around me to try to sort everything out. "Where am I, Mom?"

"We're in the ICU. You weren't responding, and you were losing oxygen really fast. Then you lost consciousness. But thank God, you're here now."

Three days prior to this incident and one week prior to high school graduation, the doctors decided to send me back to the hospital. The plan was as follows: feed me with milkshakes, prevent any movement, watch me 24/7, and then send me back into the wild. They claimed it would be a quick three days to get my heart rate back up, add a few pounds, and go home again.

A three-day hospital stay turns into six. The doctors still don't know what happened; the only slight explanation is a pre-pulmonary embolism. I think my body just wants to give up. It's tired of fighting, tired of battling the demons in its mind. Yet it's clear, too, that part of me knows it's not time to succumb to the demons.

Salmon Burgers

Salty seawater and a musty fish smell fill the air. I watch the blue, clear water twinkle outside my window. My breath slows down as I touch a finger to my thumb one at a time to calm my anxious hands.

The tips of my fingers move in circles across my thumbprint. I envision the crashing waves upon the sand. Mentally, I am by the water. I begin to feel a sense of ease here, almost restful. The timer dings, and I am instantly transported back to my reality. The fish aromas are not from saltwater seas but from our kitchen, where my mom prepares a meal I don't want.

Every night I go upstairs as my mom cooks dinner because, according to the Maudsley plan, I'm not allowed to be in the kitchen while she cooks. I dread this time because I'm convinced she's poisoning my food with butter and everything that will make me less worthy. The Maudsley plan is still in full force as I am not yet eighteen years old. My mother is in charge, and I must eat whatever she puts on my plate. In the few weeks since leaving the hospital, I have become a victim to her, my personal chef. Some may see having a personal chef as a gift. For me, it's my worst nightmare. I can usually predict what's on the menu by the aromas from the kitchen wafting up to my room. As soon as I smell fish, I know I'll soon be faced with a salmon burger.

These burgers are efficient, or so they say. This meal is chock full of Omega 3s and has the protein I need to keep nourishing my weak heart. For that reason, people call it an efficient food source, but I wonder. It feels like I have to eat a massive amount of it. The salmon burger takes up almost half of the plate. Each bite is painful, as its red, flaky substance haunts my mouth and mind. Each bite, ED tells me, will put my flat belly well on its way to reaching Santa Claus proportions again. Every other night, I am faced with this nemesis while my mom sits down and eats her salmon burger with me. We take one bite at a time, an excruciating process where my salmon burger becomes increasingly salty and wet from my tears.

"Mom, I can't eat anymore."

I know she is full too. I can tell she can barely swallow another bite. However, I will not eat alone, and she knows that if she wants me to recover, she must show me it's okay to eat, so she continues on, eating the giant burger one bite at a time. I tell her it's too much. She doesn't listen and continues on with me, slowly, delicately, compassionately. Meals often take over an hour, as tears and sometimes a full-on breakdown accompany each bite.

She reminds me of my goals. If I want to get back to movement, I will need a strong heart.

And so, I eat. After almost a month of salmon burgers, I can't bear to see another fleshy, heavy fish disk on my plate. One night my mom doesn't have a salmon burger on her plate. My emotions get the best of me; I express my outrage.

"Alz, you've got to try this on your own. I can't eat with you every night. At some point you need to know it's okay to eat. You need to do it for *you*."

How can she make me eat if she is not eating? Why do I have to punish my body with this poison if no one else does? I can't control my emotions. My tears flood down my face. My body starts to shake. I lose my mind to rage.

She wraps me in her arms. "You can do this. I know you can. If you eat this tonight, I promise you won't have to eat another salmon burger."

And so, I eat. Between each sob, I remind myself this is the last time, that I am making my heart stronger, that the torture will be over soon. I will never eat another salmon burger again.

Tadasana and Savasana

I plant my feet on a rubber mat and reach my hips toward the sky. I'm charting unknown territories. *This isn't exercise. This isn't running. This isn't enough.* I put my body through a series of poses, uncertain of how they should look or feel. I don't understand why the teacher keeps telling me to breathe. My mom moves next to me. After sixty minutes, we bow our heads to our hearts, saying "namaste," and my mom asks me how I liked it. I want to please her and tell her I love it, but I can't lie. So, I casually say, "I don't think this yoga thing is for me."

However, I return to my mat the next day. I'm currently only allowed to do this form of movement, so I come back because it's all I can do to feel slightly alive. I place a hand on my body. I connect a movement with my breath. It feels strange to be in tune with every moving part of myself. I have been at war with my body for so long. It feels uncomfortable and slightly freeing all at the same time.

In the past, I ran and ran and worked hard to escape into nothingness. I hate the idea of stillness and feeling. I still feel at home with my numbness. I didn't remember what it felt like to feel tingling sensations deep in my belly that spread through my fingers and toes. It had been so long since I felt my body physically move with free and playful power. I shut those feelings off, I thought, for my own good.

Through the various poses, standing firm like a tree or lying still on my back, I begin a dialogue with myself that sounds a little different.

My soundtrack of "you are not doing enough" slowly makes way for a breath, and the thought that "I will be okay, not today, but one day" begins to gain airplay in my mind.

With my awareness of breath and both feet planted on a yoga mat, I start to find space.

Running with Kids

"Today we are going to do an obstacle course! You get to swing like a monkey, crawl like a crab, climb a rope like Tarzan and Jane, and run through the tires of fire! It doesn't matter how long it takes you to get through. We just want you to have so much fun! Are you all ready to have so much fun?" I ask the children in front of me.

"Yes!" They scream in unison.

"Okay! Let's circle up and cheer together before we start! Who wants to lead it today?"

Five hands go up, and I spin around with my eyes closed to stop and point at someone at random. My finger lands on Joey, and we all extend our arms out in the middle. As Joey leads the phrases, we all repeat back in unison.

"I will!" he shouts.

"I will!" we call back.

"Be the best!"

"Be the best!"

"That I!"

"That I!"

"Can be!"

"Can be!"

"Fit!" he exclaims.

"Me Up!" we shout.

It's another Tuesday afternoon at Fit Me Up, the gym where I'm slowly learning how to move again. Every Tuesday and Thursday,

I coach groups of youth in fun fitness. From the "fitlets" at age three to the middle school group, we coach them on how to run with joy. We fill each day with different activities—games, obstacle courses, strength challenges, and runs. A brightly colored sign painted on the wall reminds us, "It's not about me." Despite encouraging the kids to be their best and discussing how competition can be fun, our primary goal is for all to feel welcome and joyful.

I laugh and move with the kids. Sarah, one of the seven-year-old girls, clings to my leg most days, pleading that I always do the daily activities with her. Angelina craves to be the best and always finish first. I see so much of my younger self in her. I witness movement through their eyes, not through the eyes of ED, but rather through the young girl I once was, who craved to move her body, to feel alive, to find joy amid play and freedom.

No matter how bad my day is, when I hear the kids yell "Coach Ally!" and give me the biggest hugs, I'm filled with joy. No matter how strong ED is that day, seeing them accomplish the goals they set for themselves quiets the noise of my mind and brings me right there to the present: moving with them, celebrating them, reveling in their joy.

Their parents often thank me after class, telling me how much they love coming to Fit Me Up and witnessing the joy I bring to their kids' lives. They have no idea their kids help me with my healing. They don't know that as I watch their kids celebrate their own bodies, I am learning how to love myself again. They are not aware their kids are reminding me of the little girl inside who is still in there, craving to move like a kid again—to be free.

Cycling Back to Life

I'm in a dark room filled with sweaty strangers pedaling to the beat of blasting, pumping music. A majestic and powerful woman graces the stage with an energy that makes me push through any barrier in my mind. My feet press down on the pedals. Despite my pounding heart, I feel light and full and whole. For the first time outside of a yoga room, I enter a movement environment unlike anything else I have ever experienced before.

In this sanctuary, there are no metrics or numbers to hit. There are no boards to check my progress or compare me against the other athletes there. We're just in a dark room with music all around us. It's so simple here: we do not move to change our bodies from the outside; we move to change on the inside.

Here, for the first time since my second hospital stay, I'm allowed to engage in vigorous movement. When I stepped into this room, I didn't believe in myself or my abilities. I feared my feet wouldn't be able to pedal fast enough to keep up. I didn't know if I could spin vigorously from a place of celebration instead of a place of depletion. I worried I would not belong in this new body. Jenn, the woman on stage, changed this. She cultivates a spirit of inclusivity and family in the safe space that reverberates beyond the studio. Jenn shouts her praises from the stage, instantly making us each feel connected with the other souls in the room.

Here, I begin to slowly see my body as a vessel of love within a community that lifts each other up. I begin to feel the beating of my heart again as it pounds to the rhythm of healing music. Here, I sing at the top of my lungs. Here, I begin to move again, one pedal stroke at a time. I laugh again. It's a deep laughter that comes from my belly.

One Day It Will All Make Sense

Journal Entry, April 23, 2014

(On my outlook for the day, I checked the A-Okay box.)

"I'm gonna be okay. Maybe not today. Perhaps not tomorrow. But one day I'll be okay. One day the voices in my head may tell me I'm beautiful. One day my heart will be content. One day it will all make sense. One day, maybe someday, or I can make it today. Today I'll be okay. Today I will silence the voices and remind myself I'm beautiful. Today my heart will be content. I will laugh and I will forgive. I will let go and let God."

PART 4

The Oval Park Bench

I can't do this anymore. I need help. I can't let this be my future, my forever. I want to graduate from college, and if I continue like this, I don't
know if I'll be able to. But if I say I'm not okay, then what will people
think? I told them I had recovered. They're going to say I'm the biggest
hypocrite. Besides, I was class president, I was at the top of my class, and
I was discharged from the hospital. I won an obstacle course race. I'm
fine. Yet that deep knowing inside, the one that understands more than
any outside perspective, softly reminds me I am not okay. I can't do this.
I need help. I sit on the Oval Park bench terrified as I pick up my phone
and call my mom.

  Ring . . . ring . . . ring . . . Don't pick up. If she doesn't answer, then
it's a sign I should ignore this voice inside of me and just carry on. Don't
pick up. On the fifth dial, I hear her voice on the other line. A deep
breath fills my lungs, and I sigh with relief. *Thank god you picked up.*

  I cannot speak at first. My voice is caught in the back of my throat.
My face is wet with emotion.

  "Alz, Alz, are you okay? What's going on?"

  "Mom . . . Mom . . . I . . . can't." That's all I can manage to get out
at first. I take a deep breath and attempt to carry on.

  "Alz, where are you? Are you okay?"

  "Mom, I am so sorry. I am so sorry, Mom."

  "Alz, what is going on? Honey, I love you. What's going on?"

  I can't bear to tell my parents I am not "the strong girl," that I let
them down, that I can't do this alone. I can't bear to feel the insides of

my stomach filled with the disgust of not being able to be strong on my own. My palms are sweaty, and my heartbeats are tangible, but the gentle knowing inside of me knows I must speak. For a brief instance, the small voice takes over and speaks up. *Tell her.* I lean in.

"Mom, I can't do this anymore. I need help. I just . . . I'm not okay. I don't want to keep feeling like this. I'm scared. I'm so scared. I'm so sorry. I need help."

She takes a breath that breaks the radio silence on the other side of the phone. Then all she says is "I love you."

At this moment, it's all I need. In this place of pure self-hatred, I needed someone to say, "I love you," as I can't love myself. The knots in my stomach slowly break down with the fresh breath I exhale through my body at the sound of her words. She continues on.

"We're not disappointed in you. We're so proud of you. It's okay, honey. We'll get the help we need. Tomorrow I will drive down, and we'll meet with your professors, find a place to go, and figure this out. We'll figure this out."

By the next day, my mom has helped me schedule an intake call at an adult recovery center in Columbus, Ohio—The Center for Balanced Living. She has already contacted the Ohio State University administrators to discuss how we need to proceed with classes. She reaches out to my scholars' program advisor to determine what the next steps may be. My parents arrive at the doorsteps of my dorm the next day, arms open wide so I can melt into them. The warrior by my side, embodied in my mother, carries me through. She reminds me the small knowing inside me is me. She reminds me I do not and cannot do this alone. She reminds me that although I'm not okay today, there is hope. Her strong belief in me creates a small molecule of belief I can hang onto despite the doubt and fear.

That day on the Oval Park bench, I surrendered. I acknowledged the hard truth that I can't do this alone. I let go of the notion I am supposed to be "recovered" and that recovered people can't ask for help. I embraced the idea that, despite supposedly being recovered, asking for support is the first step in healing. I invited in the flickering hope that there could be a different finish line. Later, I would let go of needing to be a finite "recovered" and accept the idea there is freedom and space in "recovering."

Most importantly, that day on the bench, I began to reclaim my life. For the first time I said, "I can't do this alone," and "this isn't the life I want to live." The smallest knowing inside of me led me to make a brief phone call to my mom that changed my life. I don't know what or why or how I decided at that moment that I couldn't carry on like this, but somehow, I knew.

Let's Try This Again

I walk into the Center for Balanced Living on a Monday morning with guarded enthusiasm. The excitement likely masks the anxiousness that is bound to come out in the following weeks. Yet the adrenaline rushes through my veins, as if it knows I will need every bit of strength I have to carry me through these next few months.

Recovery feels different when I'm not being told what to do. This time around, I have an active part in the play. It's like the first time you drive with your new driver's license, and you are no longer dependent on your parents to take you where you want to go. You now hold the steering wheel, and your foot fully presses on the pedal and the brake. Your hands are sweaty because you're new to this experience, one that feels scary and challenging and freeing all at the same time.

When I step inside the doors of the Center in September 2014, I greet my treatment team with glee. They appear a bit shocked as to why someone at a recovery center is so joyful. They seem even a bit skeptical of this joy. But for the first time since I left the hospital in July 2013, I feel a true sense of hope. This time I don't feel driven by pleasing my parents or by creating a false sense of a recovered self. I have a sense there is a real chance at recovery, that the story can have another ending, that one day I may actually be rid of the toxic voices in my head.

It's the third time trying and three months of constant hard work. It's the most challenging period of my life so far. Most days I leave the

Center drained and angry. Most days I greet my mom at our hotel room with animosity. Yet a small bit of hope carries me through, especially since *I'm* in charge now, not ED, not the doctors, not my parents. I'm ready to try this again. I am ready to take on life again, to write again, to re-vision my narrative with an ending where I'm the author, and ED is only a character that never makes it out of the final chapter alive.

Mystery Brown Paper Bags

On the first day of treatment, we enter the kitchen for lunch. When I come to the table, I find a crinkled brown paper bag with my name on it, one of many stapled shut with a white tag displaying the contents inside.

I flash back to childhood and packed lunches in brown paper bags. My lunches always included a handwritten note from my mom with words like, "You are my sunshine" and "Have a wonderful day," with a big smiley face drawn in permanent marker. These bags were often filled with turkey or salami sandwiches and Pepperidge Farm Goldfish crackers and sometimes some Teddy Grahams as a special treat. The best days included a Lunchable Pizza, the brown-bag jackpot.

However, when I see these bags on the Center's countertop, I am filled with dread instead of excitement. I had spent the summer attempting to feed myself, and here I am again, a young woman being fed by another adult. My hands shake as I struggle to walk up to the brown bag, worrying it could contain a salmon burger or some kind of mystery milkshake. One of the group therapists gently touches my shoulder and says it will be okay. Then she asks, "What do you think you need for support to eat today?"

"Maybe a time limit?" is all I manage to say.

Time is the only tool I know how to use. A time limit is a clear goal I have to complete. The ticking time bomb drowns out the racing thoughts of what I'm about to eat and that what I'm eating is completely out of my control.

"Okay. We can do that, but if there are other things you need throughout the meal, please let me know. We don't allow distractions like phones, but we do often play games if the rest of the group is interested in keeping the mood light and easy."

I nod my head, despite feeling like it's anything but okay. She walks with me to collect my bag. My eyes scan the label: *turkey sandwich with carrots, hummus, and trail mix*. My breath stills; a wave of relief washes over me.

"Is this okay?" she asks.

I want to scream. This is better than okay! I feel relieved that the paper bag is not filled with foods that will instantly send me spiraling. I give her the biggest grin. She smiles back with compassion.

"We want to keep it easy and safe for the first week. Your mom mentioned you like turkey sandwiches, so we figured this could be a good first meal. There will be more challenging foods as you progress in the program, but we'll take it slow."

I don't know if I want to cry or scream with joy or hug this person, but my entire body exhales in relief. Patient, slow, and healing with time? I can do that. The first meal is simple and easy. Not all of the mystery brown bags are as easy as the first day. Some days they are filled with a cookie or another food I had once deemed poisonous.

During my one-on-one therapy sessions with Alysia, we talk about foods that are difficult. We don't just name the food; we peel back the reasons *why* it's challenging. We talk through what nutrients it provides and what tools I can use to work through it. Over time I no longer have mystery brown bags, as I graduate into other levels of the program. I begin to create my own meals.

I start to understand why my body needs fuel and how it processes my meals. It is logical and scientific. I learn how the apple I eat will fuel my brain to think properly. I can finally see the bags are not an obstacle to overcome but to embrace. I can slowly start to accept food is not the demon; it's actually the fuel I need to fight my ultimate enemy, ED. I even start to find joy in lunches, like I once did as a young girl.

In the Family

In our hotel room, I feel surrounded by the pain between my parents and me. The noise from the TV is the only sound interrupting our silence. My brain is exhausted from a full week of treatment. I don't want to speak to anyone. My head pounds, and my eyes are heavy. My mom and dad exchange nervous glances that I catch out of the corner of my eye. My mom squeezes my dad's hand; I am perplexed as to why they stay so quiet.

My dad eventually turns down the volume on the TV.

"Hey, buddy. There's something I want to share with you."

The thoughts begin to race, and I immediately conjure up worst-case scenarios. I look at my mom's sullen face, wondering if someone has died. Or perhaps my parents are breaking up as a result of this eating disorder. I'm not used to my dad's serious tone. Whenever he's this way, it usually means something is seriously wrong. The only times I have seen him cry were when my aunt passed away and that brief glimpse of his tears when I was in the hospital. There are no tears tonight, but he seems on the verge of crying.

"What's up, Dad?"

"There's something I never shared with you because I didn't know if you would be ready. But I think it will help you heal."

I'm confused about what this information might be.

"What is it?"

"So, I get where you've been. This is why it has been so hard for me sometimes. I didn't ever think I would watch my daughter have to go through what I went through. I am really sorry."

He chokes back his emotions as my eyes swell with tears. I am beginning to register his words, yet I do not fully understand them. He continues.

"When I got out of college during my first job in Duluth, I got really thin. Although neither Nana nor I, nor a doctor, ever diagnosed it, I also had an eating disorder. I've been in your shoes, and I get it. I used to eat a can of green beans and run about ten miles a day."

The gravity of his words overwhelms me. How is he just telling me this after over a full year of my diagnosis? Why didn't he tell me sooner?

He must have read my mind.

"I know you may be wondering why I didn't tell you before, but I didn't think you were in a place to hear it yet. Now I've really seen you making strides, and with the family therapy we've been doing, I think it was finally time to share it with you."

My tears start to flow with pain, understanding, and a whole new level of connection to this man whom I've idolized for all my life. I've looked up to my dad for so long. I have craved his approval. I've wished I could find another man like him. Now we are standing, as warriors, side by side on the same battlefield.

I wrap my arms around his neck, and we cry together.

"I love you, Daddy."

"I love you too, buddy. Just know that if I can do this, I'm sure as hell you can too. Know you got me as your dad, but you also got me as someone who gets it, who understands the thoughts in your head, who knows how tough this is."

I blamed myself for so long. Since the beginning, I thought this was all my fault. I had known my aunt and cousin had a history of anorexia, but nothing compares to understanding that my own father has experienced this demon. It's so much more personal than the cultural desire to be thin. It's biological, like other diseases that pass down from generations in DNA. Knowing I have another soldier with me who not only is here to support me, but who has been deep in the trenches fighting his own fight, I find hope.

No Easy Answers

I sit between the walls of the Center, as Dr. Hale, our head resident doctor, explains that eating disorders come in many forms. I am very familiar with anorexia and know about bulimia and binge eating, but I have yet to hear of ED's spectrum. For my own ED, I have only come to know him as anorexia. Yet here I am listening to Dr. Hale explain different forms of ED. Since my initial diagnosis, there were still parts that did not make sense. Anorexia resonated with me to some degree, but it seemed it was only a fragment of the truth. Anorexia covered the lack of eating, but it did not explain my exercise compulsion and obsession with "clean eating."

She talks about different forms of ED that are considered EDNOS, eating disorders not otherwise specified. One of these EDNOS is called orthorexia. Dr. Hale begins to describe orthorexia. She explains how it's an obsession with healthy eating and a fear of "poisoning" your body if you eat something that is not "clean." She further explains it can have a component of "an obsession with exercise" and using movement to remain in an ideal state of extreme healthiness.

Orthorexia, she said, is often hard to diagnose because fitness and health are praised so heavily in our society. Exercise is often misconstrued as being only good or the epitome of health, but there can be too much of a good thing, even of exercise. I felt her words resonate with me bone-deep.

After hearing what she explained, I realized my ED has two parts: anorexia and orthorexia.

Establishing a diagnosis that makes sense to my individual experi-ence is like getting a one-time copy of the answers to the test. I can view the answers, but I can't refer to this sheet of paper during the actual test. I understand now why I am obsessed with healthy eating and why eating again to some degree may be slightly easier than others who only have an anorexia diagnosis. I also understand why the movement component is hard for me to manage. My answer for my test is I need to disassociate movement as a reward for food or a permission for my meal. I have to begin to simplify my relationship with my body. And I must continue to eat again and again. Today I still have to put in the work to employ the answers and actually take the test.

Receiving that diagnosis is not a magic pill for solving all my prob-lems, but it does provide a clearer blueprint for healing. However, just knowing what I'm dealing with is not a quick fix. The hard work has only begun.

One Day (and One Tear) at a Time

Her big eyes look at me through round glasses from across the room. White noise plays in the background as I glance at the walls. She asks me how I think I'm progressing and how my first week in treatment has been.

I've spent nine hours a day in this place for seven days now, a total of sixty-three hours with strangers who already don't feel like strangers. Still, my mask has been plastered on since I started.

Abigail, a fellow patient, shares that she is struggling during group time. I step in to offer her advice about how she can use different breathing techniques and other tips from what I've learned in my journey so far. I try to wear a superhero cape, acting like a hero that I'm not. Abigail smiles and nods, accepting my suggestions, more or less. Who am I to give advice to a forty-something-year-old who has clearly lived so much more life than I have? Even in treatment, I'm supposed to be the strong, resilient one. *Don't show you're struggling during mealtime. Don't show you're not finished recovering. Don't open up about what is going on in your mind. Don't let them see you're in the depth of ED's wrath. Tell them what they want to hear and carry on.*

I sit across from Alysia, my in-patient therapist. It's just the two of us with no group to impress. I smile and muster up some bullshit answer to explain how I am feeling.

"It's been really great. I feel like I'm progressing and making a lot of strides. I feel like I'm well ahead of where I was before, and I should probably be able to be done with treatment soon and get back to college." I pause, assuming I did a great job playing my part. My voice went up in volume and pitch. I smile. I remain calm and emotionless. She must be convinced by my performance.

However, instead of believing that performance, Alysia asks, "Do you even want to get better?"

A small corner of my mask cracks. Her question strikes me like an unexpected tree branch that smacks me right in the face without warning. My blood boils at her audacity. *How could she even ask me that question? Of course I want to get better. That's why I'm here, isn't it?* At first, I keep my thoughts private. I always aim to please others, and it's clear she isn't buying it.

"Um . . . yes . . . of course I do! I talk in group sessions, eat my food, and follow all the rules. I am getting better."

She stares back at me, silent. I try to stutter out some other statements to convince her I'm getting better. But before I can, she interrupts me and presents me with another reality.

"Allyson, you don't have to be the best at recovery. You don't always have to be the strong one or the positive one. You don't have to be the best at having an eating disorder either. I really don't think you actually want to get better."

With these words, my jaw actually drops. I'm trying so hard to be better. No one has called me out like this. Instead of responding, I go silent. I think she can sense the tension in the air. It would be impossible not to.

"I know that may come off harsh, and I do think you want to recover. But if you don't start letting people in and facing your emotions, you'll never heal. I know it can be scary, but being positive all the time isn't realistic. You're hiding how you're truly feeling, and until you actually let people help you, you won't recover."

Like a wave crashing into my body, I fall apart in a moment. My breathing is fast, and I can't catch a full breath. I feel overwhelmed by the raw emotion seeping through my veins. She looks at me with care and gives me space to finally let down my mask. She allows space to finally be messy, space to not be okay.

When I'm able to catch my breath again, all I say is "thank you." There are no other words needed to fill the silence. We have a mutual understanding that what she said finally broke the walls I've built around me. Thank you for seeing parts of me I can't even see myself. Thank you for breaking me down and seeing past my mask. Thank you for giving me space to finally heal.

The next day in the group session, I don't smile. I don't offer advice. Instead, I cry for the entire forty-five minutes, not wiping my tears but letting them be. I feel the pain slowly dripping out of the water trickling down my face, one tear at a time.

From the Inside Out

Language is at the root of my recovery story. What I once called "exercise," I now call "movement." As a young girl, I didn't exercise. I moved my body because I was excited to see my friend and feel joy turning the pedals beneath my feet. At nineteen years old, shifting the phrase from exercise to movement reminded me that movement does not always have to be hard and intense. Movement can be joyful, freeing, and purposeful to provide stress relief, aliveness, and clarity. Movement can also include a wide range of activities from running, to biking, to strengthening my body, to simple walks with friends, to dancing in the streets. Movement includes it all.

When I'm present, moving my body no longer becomes just a way to spend time and exhaust myself. Mindfulness builds intention and purpose. Now, before I move my body, my therapist challenges me to ask myself why. Why am I moving?

If I tell my therapist I want to burn calories or that I just checked my body and I have to change it, then the answer is no. I'm not allowed to move that day. My therapist might also challenge me to find my breath, journal out my thoughts, and then revisit how I'm feeling. Sometimes if my *why* is to change my body, I still move—the process is hard and slow. Yet over time, I've started to honor my why. I use my tools, I reach out for support, and I build intention into my movement.

I am running because I am celebrating the strength of my legs. I am lifting because I am gaining strength in my arms. I am practicing on my mat, so I can show up more fully for those around me and connect to myself. I walk to clear my mind after a long and stressful day. Some days I simply crave movement to feel alive.

Moving in this new way is never linear. Some days I'm sucked right back into exercising from a place of depletion. On other days, I lean into my resilience and move for joy. Like life, it's a constant process, a constant learning and relearning. There is no fast track or secret recipe. There is intentionality and purpose. There is a lot of therapy and talking it out. There is remembering where I have been and where I hope to go. But I always try to carry with me the vision of moving for joy, for the little girl who so badly wanted to love and be loved just as she was.

Reclaiming Movement

During the initial intake process at the Center, the doctor asks me why I think recovery may not have worked in the past, and how I thought we could work together to be more successful this time. I tell her movement is integral to who I am—from running with my dad, to trying all different kinds of sports, and through it all, realizing I have a craving to move my body in a variety of ways. Movement is how I feel alive, connected to myself, part of this world. Recovery will not work if I'm stripped away from my ability to move.

The intake doctor nods her head, and I expect the answer I've heard countless times before. *We know this, but you've ruined your body and your heart, so we can't allow you to move.* I expect her to say I will be confined to yoga and walks, and running will never be in my future. But she surprises me by acknowledging how important movement is to me. She says it will be a critical part of my recovery plan.

She explains how the Center has a dedicated movement plan created by a sports psychologist whose expertise is in eating disorder recovery. She explains how the movement plan will likely start slow, but that it will build over time, and how I will have a prescribed plan, just like a meal plan. I feel seen as she acknowledges the core of who I am.

As my time at the Center continues, I get my plan, a prescription to feel alive, to find joy through moving my body. The plan starts small, forty-five minutes at a time. My mom supervises these workouts to ensure I stay within the boundaries of the plan. Then, as I build trust with the sports psychologist, my therapist, and my mom—by demonstrating that

I can keep within the bounds of my overall health plan—I am able to begin moving on my own.

Within the confines of this plan, I discover freedom. Within the structure of this plan, I find strength and hope. Because of my orthorexia diagnosis, I thought I was supposed to believe that movement was the demon and that if I let it back into my life, I would instantly spiral back to ED. Before the existence of this plan, my life became confined to black and white, movement or no movement. But with support, I found peace in a gray area. I learned it was possible to follow my longing and move. It was no longer about self-depletion; I moved out of love for my body.

Mirrors

I stand in front of a mirror and feel like I'm in a funhouse. My body appears to be ten times larger in this reflection, with my legs ballooned and my arms doubled in size. The mirror shows every imperfection, every flaw, every ounce of flab on my body. I have to look away. Despite my small size, when I look in the mirror, I tell myself a different story. I fold over in half, and my belly crinkles with skin. The mirror announces this is all too much, and so am I.

When I stand at the mirror, I pick away at everything I see. I attempt to take a deep breath to calm down, but that action just expands my belly, and I can't help but fixate on that. *Look at me*, the mirror screams. I start to pick at my face, squeezing the skin on my cheeks, noting how large my pores are. I continue to stare. When I'm in front of the mirror, my brain plays tricks on my eyes. I'm hyper-focused, finding fault with all of me.

I get out of the shower and speed past the mirror to avoid looking again. I go out with friends, and I won't check to see if my outfit matches, afraid that if I look in the mirror at all, I'll be once again caught in a diatribe of hatred about my body. When shopping, I close my eyes in the dressing room, relying on my mom to give me feedback. How much time have I spent avoiding mirrors? The minutes add up.

At the Center, we do a challenge where we look at two images of ourselves, one where we can see our face, and one where it's just our body. Interestingly, when I can't see my face in the photo, I can affirm that this girl looks small and a bit unhealthy. But as soon as I am shown the same image with my face in the picture, I see every single flaw and affirm the person in the photo is disgustingly large.

In individual therapy, we work through my avoidance of the mirror. We integrate exposure therapy, as I'm challenged to spend three minutes each day looking in the mirror. Instead of critiquing my body, I'm asked to find body neutrality. Some days, body neutrality comes from looking at the mirror and stating something I like about myself, related or unrelated to my body. Sometimes I affirm my strong arms, and other days I honor my strong mind. At times, I sob standing in the mirror, tears rinsing away my pain and disgust. Once I cry and smile and feel everything in between. Over time, the mirror becomes more of a friend, though it still spews hatred from time to time.

I continue to talk about my relationship with the mirror. I begin looking at pictures with my face in them. I work to speak kindly to my body. Some days I am victorious by only spending five minutes, instead of hours, criticizing my body. On other days I sob uncontrollably, asking the mirror why she is so mean. Some days I smile, realizing I am no longer avoiding the mirror. I'm learning how to speak kindly to myself in the mirror, even for brief moments.

Adventures with My Mama

When we decided the Center for Balanced Living would be the right place for me, my mom quit her job teaching English as a second language and moved to Columbus, walking alongside me the entire way. The Residence Inn became the home for a new journey of healing, doubt, anger, connection, and love.

After eight hours of treatment, I often come back to the hotel room exhausted. The last thing I want to do is eat or talk. Even though my mom loves to talk, she respects my boundaries. We sit in silence watching TV to decompress or go for short walks to de-stress from the long day. During these nightly walks, she skips in the goofiest ways, trying her best to add joy and laughter to our time together.

In times past, I knew how to exhaust my body, but I have never before focused on sitting in my feelings, pulling back all the layers, and chipping away at my deeply rooted beliefs. My mom offers solace, grace, and compassion, even when I'm not in that space. She lets me scream, cry, and be wherever I'm at. She embarks on whatever adventure I crave to experience on the weekends, attempting to add some sense of fun and normalcy to our groundhog-like days.

Our weekends often include a trip to Patterson Fruit Farm. With the crisp fall air, we walk the pumpkin fields and spend time strolling around the farmers' market. We purchase new jams, fresh sweet potatoes, and roasted peanut butter to top our nightly desserts. My mom spends her weeks researching fun local events in the city to try to add brightness to my bleak days. We stumble upon the Great Pumpkin Festival one sunny Saturday, and my body feels full of warmth and joy all afternoon.

My mom reminds me of my strength, even when I want to give up. She asks me about my day but doesn't pry when I say I don't want to talk about it. She never misses a family therapy session, where we spend many hours crying and healing. She tells me how scared she has been and how she just wants me to get better, but that she can't fix me herself. I tell her sometimes I need more support, but other times, I want her to just listen without judgment and without trying to fix me. She still reads and researches and tries to find a solution, but with each session, we both learn there is no one simple fix.

There is only active listening and understanding; there is compassion and patience; there are our daily adventures to build the simplest forms of bliss. In these three months, my mom and I become more than mother and daughter. We become adventure partners, best friends, confidantes, sources of truth, and the truest forms of happiness, even when we don't know if joy can be found some days. She makes me see light again, when often all I see is darkness; she shows me that each day can be filled with moments of contentment, even if sorrow weaves in and out. She demonstrates that love, time, and hard work can heal anything. She makes me believe in myself again. Adventuring with my mom begins to give me back my life, a life that has been missing adventure for far too long.

Rewiring My Brain

Imagine the first time you learned how to ride a bike. You sit down on the seat, and your feet awkwardly dangle near the pedals. You struggle to keep balance while your dad holds your shoulder attempting to keep you steady. You fall as you lose your balance, and then you get up again. The next day, your dad lets go for a longer period of time, and you're able to balance, your legs pedaling as your core attempts to keep you stable. The next day you fall again. You get back up and try again.

Day by day you hardwire these movements into your body and mind. What starts as something difficult slowly turns into muscle memory, a pathway that associates movement patterns and connections between your body and mind. Soon you can ride a bike without even thinking about it.

Rewiring my brain is like trying to unlearn how to ride a bike. I sit upon this bike, and everything I thought I knew about how to ride has completely changed. I have to learn how to pedal differently. Instead of holding onto the handlebars in front of me, I have to hold onto handlebars above my head. Every hard-coded pattern needs to be stripped away and replaced by new behaviors.

My mind is habituated to neural pathways that tell me to move no matter what:

- It's nice outside—I need to go for a run.
- I'm anxious—I need to go for a run.
- I feel full—I need to go for a run.

- I'm hungry—I need go for a run.
- I feel fat—I need to go for a run.
- Someone else is running—I need to go for a run.
- I get in a fight with my mom—I need to go for a run.
- I'm happy—I need to go for a run.
- I'm bored—I need to go for a run.

Through my therapy, I realize a wide range of stimuli triggered one reaction: I felt I had to run. This response was strong and automatic. I didn't have to think about what I needed to do. I felt I knew the answer in my bones.

In my recovery, I learn about a technique called "opposite action to emotion reaction."

This is how it works: I start with a sunlit paved trail, and I feel every ounce of my body craving to go for a run. But instead of running down the path, I walk to the park and read in the sun. Despite my discomfort, I lean into the opposite reaction and sit. I take a deep breath. My head is full of thoughts. As I continue to sit, my head begins to clear, and I start to feel more comfortable with each breath I take.

The anxiousness and fullness pathways are harder to rewire. The desire to run when I feel anxious and full is much stronger than a trigger of sunshine. I am so used to running to calm my mind that sitting in the stillness with anxiousness and fullness feels like pins and needles that only get increasingly painful. But I know that if I don't try the opposite action to these emotional reactions, I will never rewire my brain. So, even amid the discomfort, I breathe and sit.

Some days I know it's okay to move. But I need to keep working, rewiring, and rebuilding my new bike.

Over and over again, I remind myself this is not forever, and movement is still critical to who I am. Eventually I learn to embody authentic movement balanced with stillness. I move side to side and front to back. I sit quietly, in happiness, sorrow, and everything in between. I move with joy and anger. My body can respond to it all.

The Power of AND

I want to recover, AND it's too hard.

I want to exercise, AND I don't think I can do it in a healthy way.

I am hopeful, AND I'm really scared.

I am resilient, AND ED is strong.

Life isn't a series of one truth and one lie. It's a series of gray, a series of holding space for two forces that may seem opposing *and* can both be valid. I learn about the power of AND during group therapy at the Center. It's the simplest shift of phrases and one of the most powerful of shifts to my ongoing energy and life today.

AND shows me I can feel multiple feelings at once, think multiple thoughts, love multiple people, and feel at home in multiple places. Now there is an opening in the gray, a space to live in a spectrum, to live in this place where multiple words can hold truth. At the very same moment, I can feel strong AND scared. I can feel the tingling, nervous sensations in my fingertips AND simultaneously feel the power of my legs carrying me through.

AND also provides me with the freedom to not always need an answer, to live in the presence of the before AND the after. This way of feeling my way into the in-betweens of living provides healing, discomfort, AND everything in between.

For today, I am whole, and I am slowly piecing the depth of my soul back together. I am worthy, and I am learning to negate what no longer makes me feel worthy. I am strong, and I am allowed to struggle. I am loved, and it's tough to feel loved sometimes. I am independent, and I can ask for help. I am slowly releasing ED, and some days, I miss him. This is where I am, and I am becoming someone new, headed somewhere I have not been before.

Leaping into the Wild

We wrap up our final family therapy session at the Center. Since it's mid-December, we discuss holiday times and how to prepare for festive gatherings. We talk about setting up signals for moments we're in distress or need support. We talk through potential situations, people, or food that may be triggering, and how to navigate those moments. We also talk about how this will be hard, and if the holiday season feels a bit different this year, that's okay. We are empowered to set boundaries and ask for what we need. We are encouraged to bring our own food if it will help us be present or incorporate other tools we've discussed to help us navigate the already stressful holiday season. My mom and I determine my safe word will be me sharing that I need some fresh air or asking to go for a walk. If words are hard, I can also use a slight tap on her shoulder to signal I may need some support or time away.

Despite all my adventures with my mom, I feel like this is the first time I'm truly leaving the bubble. I worry about the triggers in the outside world. My body is flooded with so many racing thoughts. What will my relatives think? If they ask about Ohio State, how will I respond? How do I explain the process of rewiring my brain? Will they comment on my "healthy" body? Will they applaud me for eating food again?

I don't know the answer to any of these questions. I do know that for three-and-a-half months, I have processed, healed, and developed tools for coping in the world. I have done the work. Now it's time for me to graduate. After the holidays, I won't be returning to the Center and meeting up with my fellow warriors who so thoroughly understand my mind. From now on, I will only be returning for outpatient therapy.

But what will it be like to return to civilian life? Will I have enough support at Ohio State? Should I switch schools to be closer to home? What will I feel about living in the dorms again? Will I be able to handle school and extracurricular activities? Will I relapse? Will I ever fully recover?

I have all those fears, but I also have confidence. I know I've gained strength I didn't have before. I can shout from the rooftops how I've learned to move in healthy ways. I've grown in ways I could never have imagined.

In our final meeting, I hug Alysia, Dr. Hale, and the others one last time. My face is damp with emotion. They all tell me they're proud of me. They say they know I'll be fine. Abigail gives me a book to remind me of my unique strengths, and we hold each other in a tight embrace as the tears flow.

I take a deep breath as my mom squeezes my hand and tells me she loves me. It has not fully sunk in that I am going out into the wild. I don't fully realize this is just the beginning of the healing process. I do know I'm brave and resilient, and for now, it's enough to trust the world is filled with life beyond my current understanding.

Triggers

At the Center, every ounce of my universe was controlled. I was part of a bubble in which I was shielded from the potential dangers of the outside world. During the program, I wasn't allowed to wear tight clothing, since showing too much of my body could potentially trigger others. We never spoke in numbers. Numbers can trigger. We didn't use certain words: healthy, clean eating, and detoxes. If we wondered if our words would upset others, we had to consult our individual advisors before sharing them with the group. We were sensitive, at-risk, and impressionable. All outside forces must be controlled.

Once I am released back into the wild, I try to create my own version of the protected universe I had during the program. I ask my parents and my family never to talk about numbers, food, movement, or bodies around me. When my dad states he is going on his run and that he just ate some junk food, I lash out, telling him he is not abiding by the new rules. He tells me I need to calm down and learn how to deal with other people.

I don't understand how to live in this new world filled with triggers. I don't understand why other people can't avoid triggering me. I am now in a place where I can't control others. Their triggers create feelings that make me want to completely crumble, spiral, or cry. But now I know I can only control my reactions. I can take this information and start to heal my wounds.

The triggers in the wild feel endless, and so is my breath. I slowly recognize the obsession with trying to control the wild is only adding to the weight of my chains. I slowly remember the tools I built at the Center—use my four-seven-eight breathing method, tap my fingers to my thumb, walk away, write out my thoughts, cry it out, scream it out, move my body with ease, go for a walk, go for a run sometimes, drink some water, and take a deep breath. Slowly the triggers loosen their grip, and my internal locus of control becomes stronger. Slowly I breathe, cry, laugh, scream, and release.

You Can't Sit (Live, Be) Here

It's my first week back at school. We sit in the Ohio State Student Union Auditorium waiting for a seminar to begin as I try to make small talk with my old roommates. I try to remember what it's like to discuss things other than how to rewire your brain, why seeing someone running is triggering, and why eating an apple will help my brain process and learn. I forget what it's like to have normal conversations. I remember growing up with my mind that always seemed to race ahead, unable to connect with the kids at the playground. They talked about how cute Jack was and how stupid the math homework was, and I just wanted to discuss the meaning of heaven. Now, at this moment in the auditorium, I remember that feeling of being unable to connect, that feeling that I don't belong.

I sit with Nikki and Katlynn and Elizabeth, my roommates from the prior semester. When I return from the Center at the start of the second semester, I move into a different room to have more space and ideally less triggers. As we sit in the Student Union, the topic of where everyone is living next year is brought up. They bring up the subject quietly, as if they want to play a game of telephone where no one calls me. I don't know the entire string of words. I attempt to intercept the game and ask where everyone is living.

Nikki clams up and fumbles over her words. She is the people pleaser and peacekeeper of the group; she hesitates to share the truth. Katlynn dances around the question, until Elizabeth finally states they all have their options lined up, and there isn't any room for me. Another sophomore overhears the discussion and pipes up, saying she thought there was one spot still open where Katlynn and Nikki were planning to live. After this comment, I hear radio silence static that I want to turn off and stop the pain, but it permeates the room. Nikki and Katlynn look at one another, flushed, and then back at the sophomore who spoke up, then regretfully, back at me.

"Oh yeah," Katlynn says. "I think we have someone to fill it though. Sorry, Allyson."

Despite taking a semester off, I ventured back to campus during the weeks when I was able to do so and visited on some of the weekends. I didn't think it would be out of the question to be considered in future housing plans, especially since we had talked about it in prior conversations. Where and who you were going to live with is similar to who you were going to sit with at the lunch table in middle school—life or death.

Life with a girl like me is death to them. I find out later from someone else in the program that the resounding consensus is they don't want to live with a girl with an eating disorder. Once again, I'm too much, too "messed up," or not enough.

Sweatshirt Sizes

It's a Monday night in the dorm room as I attempt to fill out the order form for our sorority's apparel order. I open and close the Google form numerous times. I scroll through the list of names, checking the sizes the other girls are getting. LoLo—*small*, worthy. Megan—*large*, unworthy. I don't want to be Megan. I close my laptop, with no size marked yet.

I can't get myself to write down a size. I badly want to order a medium, but I'm terrified of what it will mean. How will that define me? Will the other girls think less of me?

It's the last day to write my size down. The agony of marking down my size for the rest of the sorority to see has consumed me for two weeks. My mind will not let go of the worthiness scale it has identified in a letter on a tag. What may take someone thirty seconds to fill out has taken me weeks.

I ask my Big Sister what size to get, hoping this will help me overpower my racing thoughts. She replies simply, "Up to you! I usually get medium or large."

A straightforward response without conditions. No other qualifications of "I like it oversized" or a deep rationale for why she ordered a certain size.

I mark myself down for a small, close my laptop, and cry quietly. When will I get to a place where I can pick a sweatshirt size without it taking two weeks? When will I be able to let go of the need to compare myself to other women and their bodies?

The next time sweatshirt orders go out, I order a medium. It only takes one week this time to write it down. I justify my order with "I like it oversized." I explain this answer to the other girls at our chapter dinner. Some nod or politely agree, yet no one truly cares. The next time, I get a medium again, without any justification.

No magic switch gets me to this place. There are hundreds of moments of rewiring my brain. There are deep breaths. There are words written in journals about processing emotions and filling the emptiness inside me with something other than numbers and letters.

Coffee Shop Comfort

Dates, almond slices, chickpeas, roasted chicken, avocado, and the most delicious dressing: I crave this village salad always. It's safe and easy. I know what to expect, since this is a meal I had at the Center during one of the days the team brought in food from the outside world. I know how this salad will nourish my body. I eat this salad at least two or three times each week. It's part of my weekly routine: go to Northstar, order the village salad (dressing on the side), then go to Mission Coffee across the street (order the weekly specialty coffee), and study.

These days are filled with so much joy and ease. I love to challenge my mind and process all the information I have absorbed in class. I reread all my notes, make flash cards, write my own twenty-five-page exams to prepare for the actual exam, and people watch. I spend afternoons writing or reading for fun. It's time away from the sorority house, from the trigger-filled world of body talk and constant comparison.

This routine is my version of the Center. I create my own bubble to prevent triggers from the outside world. If I know exactly what I am eating, I can silence the running thoughts of ED attempting to calculate the calories or the amount of macronutrients (proteins, carbs, fats) of everything I put in my body. These calculations are a hard-coded pathway that's still impossible to turn off. Without trying, I can look at a plate and calculate the amount of energy it entails. By eating the same salad every day, I can turn off my brain's FitnessPal.

Despite these afternoons filling my days with respite, I also avoid most human interactions. Amid the perceived comfort and ease, I am slowly losing "me" again. I convince myself I don't want to have a normal college experience. I just want to study and go to coffee shops. I tell myself that despite choosing Ohio State largely because it's a football school, I don't like football anymore. I say to myself that I will graduate in three years because I am over the whole college scene. I am healing in coffee shops. I don't need a village; I only need village salads.

Part of it's healing. Part of it's hurting. Part of it's recovering. Part of it's pretending. Part of it's soul-giving. Part of it's soul-taking. Part of it's gaining. Part of it's diminishing. Here, I lose myself and I find myself.

Building My Village

It's the spring semester of my sophomore year, and I'm talking with my academic advisor, Lindsay, discussing what I need to graduate next year. She asks me why I want to graduate in three years.

"Is it because of financial reasons? Are you really ready to graduate?"

I tell her how the whole "college scene" isn't for me and that I'm ready for the working world.

I don't tell her that since leaving the Center and coming back to Ohio State, I still feel so lost. While it seems everyone is out partying, making friends, and having the best time of their lives, I'm working to rewire my brain and control the endless triggers around me. I'm trying to live and cope while preventing a relapse. I believe leaving college is the answer to recovery.

She starts to dig deeper into my desire to leave. She asks me about my time spent in Delta Sigma Pi, a business fraternity, before I left for the Center. "Would you consider going back there? What else brings you value?"

I pause and look around the room. When I think of returning to Delta Sigma Pi, I feel anxious and unsure. I don't know if I would be accepted or welcomed back. I gently nod and tell her I could consider it. I then look back at the list of goals I wrote in my old journal during freshman year before leaving for the Center.

1. Graduate Summa Cum Laude.
2. Become a Pace Setter (a prestigious award given to the top 1 percent of junior and senior business students based on grades and involvement).
3. Get into Delta Sigma Pi.
4. Become a Peer Advisor to mentor younger students.

I feel anxious looking at this list because I know that once again my dreams may be taken away by a deeper fear inside of me. But I remember that day on the Oval Park bench when I called my mom. A small, knowing voice inside of me tells me to show Lindsay my list and talk through the possibilities. This voice lets me know maybe it isn't time to give up yet.

Then I think about what brings me value. I don't know yet. I'm still trying to disassociate my worth from exercise and food. I do know this list includes goals I would regret not chasing if I just gave up, graduated college early, and let ED win yet again. So I share these goals with Lindsay, and we begin to discuss how I could get there. If I want to be a Peer Advisor and a Pace Setter, I will need to be more involved in school activities. It would make sense to return to Delta Sigma Pi. I leave Lindsay's office with a plan to go after my goals.

I slowly start to focus my attention on the list. It feels invigorating to focus on other things besides food, movement, and studying. I start to let myself be open to the possibility of embracing college and the remaining time, despite feeling like ED took away my first two years.

I spent so much of the first part of college in quasi-recovery that I never let myself fully experience all that was happening around me. Instead, I vacillated between feeling like who I wanted to be and who I used to be, never letting myself be who I was in that moment—healing, recovering, growing.

When I return to Delta Sigma Pi, I begin to feel what it's like to have "a village" around me. I let myself form deeper connections with people I meet and let current friends in more. I achieve my goals of Pace Setter and Peer Advisor.

Adventure Again

We're going to the Fiesta Bowl! My roommates buy tickets and invite me to join them on this excursion. Instantly my mind is flooded with worries. The last time I was on a flight was to Europe right before my diagnosis. I have not yet let myself travel or go on any typical college spring break trips. My trips consist of monthly drives between Columbus and Cleveland.

If I go on this trip, how will I get my workout in? What kind of food will we be eating? I try to talk myself off the ledge: Breathe deep. It's only five days. I can do this. There is more to life than routines and control.

My mind vacillates back and forth between ED still creeping in saying, *You're not ready*, to my wise mind saying, *Take that risk. You can do this.* I call my mom to act as my voice of reason.

When my thoughts are spinning fast, sometimes her reassurance reminds me of my strength. We talk through the details of the trip and how I can build a plan for success. I can find structure in planning out some mindful movement and bringing snacks I know are safe and filling. We build out my toolkit, and I agree to go, knowing she will only be a phone call away.

I never tell my roommates I have not flown since I was seventeen. I do not tell them that despite the mask of confidence, I am a bundle of fear. I pack my bags with my journal, some safe snacks, and my worry stone. I pack my mental toolbox, reminding myself of all I can tap into: four-seven-eight breathing, my dialectical behavioral therapy skills, a text to my mom, and my inner mantras that tell me over and again I can do this. I book my tickets, excitedly anxious to embark on this adventure.

Once we arrive, I feel my senses stimulated as I soak in new places, sights, and even enticing foods. We climb a mountain, watch our Ohio State team lose to Clemson, and make the best of New Year's Eve, despite the loss, with wild adventures at night. I text my mom a few times but not as often as I expected, as my anxiety is dimmed by the noise of adventure.

When we are out at dinner, I order sweet potato fries and a southwest chicken salad. It is both safe and freeing. The sweet potato fries challenge me, while the chicken salad provides me with fuel I'm familiar with. I lean into knowing I do not have to jump full into adventure, overwhelmed by either going all-in or not at all.

I move my body in the mornings with light runs in the city and remind myself I can still incorporate a sense of normalcy and routine amid the newness and unfamiliar territories. During these runs, I take in the red rock and mountain views, my senses heightened, the noise of needing to push harder quieting.

This short trip creates a new craving in my body and mind. I want to find expansion and lean into a wide-open world I have yet to explore. With this trip, I see I can adventure again. I can fly on a plane and not return to a hospital bed. I can get out of my comfort zone. This adventure begins to revive the parts of me that have been turned down for so long.

It shows me there are different ways of being. When I'm confined to the chains of ED, I'm only allowed one way. I find freedom and possibility adventuring again, opening my eyes to a world where I can belong without ED.

During my final two years at Ohio State, I begin to heal into all I am becoming. I now spend my weekends tailgating and cheering in "the Shoe," lit up by the infectious energy of 100,000 people rooting for the Buckeyes. On weekdays, I connect again with other humans and slowly build my village. In senior year, the year I almost missed, I take trips to Nashville and spend my spring break exploring the streets of Los Angeles. At night I dance on our apartment tables or engage in karaoke, where we sing at the top of our lungs.

When I feel the deepest forms of joy, I send selfies with friends to my parents. My dad responds with, *Buddy, it's so good to see you finally living again.* Living again begins to feel incredible and not because I'm doing it alone. This time I am surrounded by humans who see me and love me as I am. I let them in. We push one another to go after big dreams, without losing sight of the little moments in the pursuit. We enjoy the simplest moments. It takes these moments, big and small, for me to see that dancing through life alone is not the road I want to take.

Live Like Nana

I sit at the restaurant table, almost desperately thin again, exhausted and depleted. I am supposed to be happy, thriving, and ready to have the best night of my life. It is the eve of my twenty-first birthday, and I feel anything but joy. I don't know the last time I ate a full day of meals. My toolkit goes out the window, and survival mode turns on. ED has taken over again.

During the past month, we've taken trips to and from Cleveland, fueled by calls of "It's her time. We think she's finally letting go." Each time I prepare myself to say goodbye to my beloved nana. Yet each trip is a false alarm and my nana, Joan, slowly comes back to life with our arrival. I continue to wade in anxiety and restriction, my old coping mechanism.

I attempt to eat chips and salsa at my birthday dinner, as my phone lights up with the message, "I am so sorry to hear about the loss of your nana." My heart collapses along with my entire body, as I release an uncontrollable flood of tears. A night that is supposed to be joyful has now become heartbreaking. I am supposed to be excited about this new milestone year, a coming of age, and instead I am consumed by utter grief of losing my best friend. I call my mom.

"Why did you tell me? Why did you tell me tonight?"

At that moment I am not supportive of the deep grief my entire family must be feeling. I am too consumed by my own selfish ideals of celebration. My mom apologizes because I'm not supposed to find out. My dad is one of five, and the entire family is gathered together in Ohio, except for my one aunt who does not get the memo to shield me from this information for now.

I spend the rest of the night attempting to dance and drink, but I'm drowning in my heartbreak. She lived a good, full life, they say. I can understand this sentiment, but this loss is still not easy.

I get to one of our local bars, The O Patio. At this point, most of my friends have gone home. But I see Steve, my major crush from Delta Sigma Pi, and he gives me the biggest hug.

"Oh my god, Allyson! Happy birthday! How are you?"

At this question, I completely lose it and begin sobbing. He holds me tighter.

"Oh no, what's wrong?"

"I just lost my nana a few hours ago. She was my best friend."

I feel safe in his arms as he holds me tighter. We move over to a bench on the patio, and he spends the next two hours listening to me reminisce about my nana. As I tell him about her, I am reminded of the incredible woman she was.

I describe how my nana told me all her travel stories. She always returned with colorful bracelets or other souvenirs for my sister and me, and while these gifts were wonderful, I truly cherished her stories. I tell him how I always looked at her in awe, hoping one day I would feel like I had lived such a magnificent life. As I continue to tell him these stories, I remember how my nana demonstrated what it meant to go out of her comfort zone and take hold of life. She relayed the importance of doing whatever her heart desired. She followed the paths that seemed to call her, regardless of others' opinions.

Steve smiles and wraps me in a warm hug as I continue to share stories of growing up with Nana. I would go over to her home, and we would sit at the piano for hours. Her delicate fingers touched the keys as they gently created sweet melodies. I told him about our shopping sprees. We always had to stop at Talbots, even though I hated Talbots, but I went because I knew it made her happy. Our days always ended at the Cheesecake Factory, where we made sure we ordered the brown rye breadbasket and a delicious slice of Adam's Peanut Butter Cup Fudge Ripple cheesecake. She embraced my vivacious attitude, and as I grew older, she joked with me about my latest boys and gossip. She was always a voice of reason.

I tell him how she was my best friend as tears fall from my eyes. In those moments, I know how lucky I am that I was blessed with her as my nana. I will always remember one of the last moments during my last trip to Cleveland. She was becoming increasingly tired, but she gently opened her eyes for a brief moment and looked up at me. "You're so pretty," she said. She gave me the unconditional approval and acceptance I was so hungry for before I was able to give it to myself.

My nana was beautiful from the tips of her fingers to the smile on her face and the depth of her soul. I seek to embody her adventure, zest, class, and love as I carry on through this world. In endings there are also new beginnings. On that night of a brand new year, reminiscing on all she was, Nana inspires me to begin again, embodying her essence.

Meatballs on Tuesday

His hands meticulously move in a circular motion as he rolls the red meat with the toasted bread, parsley, and basil. His brow furrows as he is focused on rolling out the perfectly shaped meatballs. Aromas of garlic and roasted tomatoes fill the air as I am transported back to my mom's kitchen and Pasta Nights.

I am in the kitchen with the same man, Steve, whom I poured my grief out to on the bar's picnic bench on my twenty-first birthday. We have been dating for a few months now. I am so intrigued by this person who helps me explore everything that may be possible in an expansive world. On one of our first dates, we go out for brunch. It's the first time I let myself eat food without feeling I need to earn it with a workout beforehand.

We are now making meatballs in my kitchen, and I am trusting in someone else to cook for me, not because I am forced to but because I crave this experience. It has been six years since I've touched red meat. I don't like it because it tastes like metal, I claim. My mind's soundtrack constantly repeats that red meat is poison.

Despite my shaking hands, I want to try these meatballs. Part of me wants to impress this new man in my life, as my people-pleasing is heightened by our relationship. Still another part of me wants to prove to myself that this red meat isn't poisonous, that I will not die by eating this red meat, and that I can take this step in recovery. So I sip the glass of red wine, slightly taking off the edge, grab a small portion of the red meat mixture and begin to roll. He comes up behind me. He places his hand on mine as he shows me how to roll the perfect meatball. In Italian culture, there is a science to every meal you create. It's not just food for fuel. There is precision and thought and love and tender care in every dish.

He is aware of my struggles, but he doesn't know it all. I'm afraid that if he knows everything, he will see me only as the girl with the eating disorder, but he doesn't. He doesn't know what a big deal it is for me to even be touching red meat. He doesn't have any idea how much of a challenge it will be for me to eat this food. Dan + Shay plays in the background as he pulls me away from rolling the meatballs and we dance. He spins me around and then pulls me in with a delicate kiss on my forehead. I am consumed by the way he looks deeply into my eyes. Here is this man who does not know the old me and all the places I have been. Here, too, is someone who sees food as a masterpiece rather than as the Devil, a poison. He guides me into understanding that food can be fulfilling and that dancing in the kitchen between glasses of red wine and garlicky tomato aromas is what living free may be like.

I hold back my tears as I feel emotion welling in my eyes. Instead I focus on his calming presence as we continue to roll the meatballs, joking at the precision of his work, everything one uniform size, while mine completely vary. We stir the sauce and place the baked meatballs in the simmering spices and tomatoes and continue to dance. I feel at peace and available to talk about life and our interests. I ask him how he learned to love cooking.

He shares how he started cooking at three years old with his nonna and mom. His mind is consumed by every piece of the recipe. It's like a mathematical equation. He explains the perfect ratio of acids to bases and how certain spices and ingredients interact with one another. His face lights up every time he talks about food. He feels pure joy, while I feel resentment and fear. However, hearing his stories and seeing the delicate love he puts into every dish, every chop of garlic, every stir of the sauce, I see food can be more than punishment. I am enthralled with his passion. Maybe I can learn a small piece of it in time.

The timer dings, and I am pulled out of the daze of enchantment and back to reality that soon I will be consuming red meat. I feel my heart begin to race like the thoughts in my mind. He plates the food, grinning from ear to ear. I take another sip of wine, assuming it will help calm my shaking hands. We sit down at the candle-lit table with fresh glasses of red wine.

He looks at me with anticipation. "Dig in!" he says.

Every fear in my body elevates. The gut-wrenching feeling I should not eat intensifies. Yet his authentic grin and his palm on top of mine gives me the power I need to try it. I take a bite, and all my anxiety is overpowered by the delicious flavors of garlic, oregano, and tomato. My taste buds light up. I enter a food experience unlike any other. This must be what they talk about—that food can be joyful. He looks at me, waiting for what I will say.

"Wow, Steven, this is amazing!"

His furrowed brow instantly turns into deep smile eye lines.

"Oh, I am so glad! I was nervous."

"I do have to share that this is big for me. I haven't had red meat in six years. And this is so good." I feel unsure of what his reaction may be.

His face turns from joy to utter delight. I see a tear slightly form in his eye as he squeezes my hand even tighter.

"Wow, Allyson. I had no idea. I'm so glad I was able to give you this experience."

I am too. Steven's kitchen, my safe haven. A girl with an eating disorder and a boy who loves to cook—what a pairing that could be. It's as if the universe knew that another being needed to show me food could be an experience, filled with the freedom to eat and dance.

And as the years continue, so many of our days are measured by food, table talk, and our connected understanding over the experience of tasting every ingredient. Together, it was no longer swallow and forget; it became more like taste, love, feel, and experience. Table talks show me food is more than anything I ever imagined it could be—it's a unifying power, a masterpiece, a way to show you care and love. Meatballs on a Tuesday night start a path of learning, deepening, caring, and loving.

At Home on My Mat

We take a deep collective breath and bow our heads to our hands to close out another Wednesday night yoga practice. My yoga teacher, Nicole, shares the weekly announcements. Usually, she tells us news about an upcoming community class or event, but tonight she announces there will be a new 200-hour yoga teacher training beginning in two months. At the sound of her words, the deep knowing inside of me instantly says *yes*.

During the past two years, Balanced Yoga has become a place of refuge and discovery. A ten-minute drive down High Street, this place with its inviting white walls and wooden floors provides a much-needed break from the typical college scene. I have spent many sacred hours at Balanced, practicing at least a few times a week. Although I now can move my body in more ways, I find that yoga continues to heal me. It's a time for me to connect my breath to movement, to let go of the racing thoughts, and to continue to deepen the connection with my body. My practice has evolved so much since the first time I stepped into a yoga room during my early stages of recovery at seventeen. I no longer crave to always do the poses perfectly or push with intensity. Instead, I find ease and balance, as I learn from a variety of teachers. I begin to discover what it means to find nonattachment, letting go of what my body or life used to look like, and embracing what is right here and now.

The further I get into recovery, the more I understand how integral movement is to me and how much its meaning has shifted. My practice continues to show me how to move in ways that add to my life and my body instead of moving from a place of depletion or punishment. I learn that others, like those I met at the Center and during my group recovery sessions at Ohio State, also struggle with finding balance in movement.

Since yoga has been so powerful in my life and with the continued progress in recovery, I want to support others in their healing. I sign the paperwork the next day without a second thought.

The first weekend we learn more about the commitments of the training, including daily practices, varying the types of practice, daily journaling, weekly homework assignments, and more. This list does not feel daunting because there is nowhere else I'd rather be. It feels exciting. Within the first weekend, I understand that while I went in with the intention to learn how to teach others and support their journey, my own path is about to be completely changed.

The first weekend, I stand in front of my fellow trainees and teachers and read a passage from *Journey into the Heart*. I am asked to share how that passage lands with me. Instantly I am overcome with a wave of emotion. The passage is about being enough just as I am. It's as if the universe knows I need to hear this passage. As I begin to share, I open up about my eating disorder and how I am slowly learning to disassociate my worth from how much I move, what I eat, what my body looks like, what grades I get, and what accolades I receive.

Nicole digs deeper and asks me what enoughness truly means to me. I can't answer her yet. I tell her I do not know, and that my intention during these next 200 hours is to discover what it means.

By the final weekend, we are challenged to do a blindfolded practice. It's scary when I can't see where my feet are planted or if I correctly place my arms over my head in Warrior One. Yet behind the darkness of the blindfold, I find the deepest connection to myself. I am forced to trust my body. I am challenged to feel every single part of it, my toes pressing down into the mat while my arms lift up strongly. During these ninety minutes, I am overcome by emotion many times, from deep laughter in falling out of a pose to the tears dripping down my face at the reminder of my imperfect humanness. In this practice, I allow myself to be messy and real.

The theme of enoughness continues to play in my mind. I allow myself to keep asking what this truly means to me. It's not an instant epiphany but, rather, a compilation of the thousands of tiny moments throughout the 200 hours. We lie in final relaxation at the end of the practice. I rest both hands on my belly, feeling my lungs fill up with air and then empty out. Instead of *enough* playing in my mind, the word *worthy* takes its place. I shake as I inhale the word "worthy" over and over again.

At the end of the training, we are all asked to share what it was like. When the circle gets to me, I again can't speak, overcome by emotion. I let myself feel it all as the others patiently hold space for me. Once I can speak, I share that I have discovered an answer to Nicole's original question during the first weekend of training.

"Enoughness for me is knowing I am worthy. I am worthy of the deep breaths and rest. I am worthy of treating myself kindly. I am worthy of an adventurous, full life. I am worthy and whole and enough."

As I look around the circle, they are all smiling back at me, a few with tears. Maggie, one of the other trainees, grabs my hand, while Nicole gives me the most empowering and welcoming hug. "I am so incredibly proud of you," Nicole says as a few tears fall down her face. I take a deep breath. They all clap, and I revel in this bliss.

I graduate from my 200-hour teacher training completely open, finally believing in my worthiness. Now I am ready to step into my own power. I want to create spaces for each person as they are—enough, whole, and worthy.

PART 5

Jumping into Life

Three, two, one—I lean to the side, let go, and jump. My heart beats rapidly, and the purest form of energy radiates through me. I am falling and flying at once; the tandem jumper taps my hands as I expand my arms out wide, opening my heart to all that this jump represents. I always thought I was afraid of heights. It was another story I told myself. Being an anxious child, I fed off my mother's worries. She is terrified of heights to the point where her breath catches in the back of her throat, and she shudders with anxiety. As an empath, when I see heights, I feel I cannot breathe either.

Why not embrace this fear I thought I had head on? Why not take a risk? Why not feel my heart beating out of my chest, my belly dropping deep into the pit of my stomach? Why not see the world from the highest views?

The moment I step out of that airplane and begin falling through the crystal blue sky, it's as if every other fear begins to fade out of view, making way for a deeply rooted sense of purposeful living. My hands and body shaking, I am still choosing to move on. With my mind racing, I can still breathe fully. I free-fall for what seems like an endless amount of time. Then instantly, the parachute breaks the fall as I grasp hold of the ends of the parachute. I am supported by the freedom of flying over the world. The breeze touches my skin as I laugh deeply and fully. I cannot stop grinning with a mix of disbelief and expansiveness as we land on the ground. My body tingles with joy.

When I jump out of that plane, it feels like letting go of so much of the fear and resistance I have been carrying. Fear of change. Fear of unknowns. Fear of the what-ifs. After that jump, I find it easier to make decisions. I remember, *I jumped out of a plane. I can get uncomfortable. I can feel shaky and scared and still move forward.* To me, this jump starts an uphill trend of facing fears, leaving my comfort zone, and embodying what it means to be and feel alive.

It also shows me that although I won't be jumping out of airplanes every day, I can still face my discomforts, even if it's in the smallest ways. I can continue to explore what life without ED may feel like. I can sit in the messiness and the stillness. I can process waves of emotions that come up again and again. I will land on my feet, a new type of parachute on my back, ready to fly.

The Mountains Call Me Home

I am on top of the world, awake and excited, as ease floods my spine and limbs. I see the mountaintops and crave feeling my feet planted firmly in their dirt, to dance beneath their trees, to view the world through the peaks of their expansive homes.

The mountaintops are lusciously green, seemingly without end. Growing up in Ohio, I had never seen earthly statues so grandiose that they make you feel infinite and miniscule all at once. I had never witnessed the world beyond the views of industrial skyscrapers. The Cleveland Clinic's seventeenth floor views are now specks of dust compared to the vastness of the mountaintops.

I am on top of Horsetooth Rock with my friend Emma during my first trip to Colorado after graduating from Ohio State. I am spending the summer exploring, wandering, finding, and growing.

We look out over the clear blue reservoir that's juxtaposed with the red, orange, and green hues that decorate the mountains surrounding our bird's-eye view. I inhale and exhale the most freeing breath I have ever taken. I close my eyes, place my hands on my heart to feel it beating, and slowly blink them open. My mind feels open and clear as I take in another breath. I am nothing and everything all at once.

My body connects with the mountains. On top of the rock, I am reminded that life is meant to constantly evolve and expand. The mountain's roots are meant to be traversed and carved. The mountain does not apologize for being too large; it just becomes larger and says, *Take me in, stand on my peaks, soak in all that is*. The mountain does not hide its scars or boulders. Instead, it opens them up and invites me in to touch them and understand why they have made the mountain stronger.

Although it will take a few years to get back to these Colorado mountains, I know one day they will be my home. Like the mountain, I am vast and expansive. On top of its strong foundation, I am accepted, and I belong.

Twentysomethings

Four months after graduation, I am walking along Lake Road in my new neighborhood in Lakewood, Ohio. I just finished cooking dinner for one, a roasted vegetable salad that is a safe food once again. I am not in a totally different city, only a fifteen-minute drive from my hometown, yet I crave to have some sense of newness.

Most of my friends have left and spread their wings, but I have chosen to remain. I am scared to know what else might be out there. I am overwhelmed by the daunting expanse of opportunity. Staying feels safe.

I take in the breeze on my skin. The cool, late summer night air fills my lungs. I take a deep breath. *Aren't I supposed to have this all figured out by now? Will I ever dream again? Will I be stuck in Ohio at American Greetings forever?* This past summer of travels showed me what expansion could look like, but it was only temporary. *Will I ever be strong enough to take a risk on me and embrace that expansive life fully?*

I remember being ten years old and thinking my twenties would be a time of certainty. I would have my entire life figured out. I would be a married twentysomething CEO. But here I am, a twentysomething drowning in uncertainty.

The autonomy I once thought I had over my life dissipates. A sea of opportunities that all feel unattainable now consume me. Choosing what food to eat and what food is okay to put in my grocery cart starts to seem miniscule compared to choosing what I want to do with my life.

In this vast world, I am overwhelmed. My doubt is still rooted in the fear I did not do enough, and I am not doing enough. I also pause and notice I have been in these places of uncertainty before. I didn't know if I could start recovery again. I didn't know if I could ever move my body for anything other than for punishment. But each day I am choosing to recover, to go to dinner with friends, to move because I want to, not because I have to. With these choices, I continue to become connected with myself.

With these choices, I am reminded of my younger self who had so many desires. For the past few years, my desires have been muted, consumed only by needing to choose recovery each day and trying to silence my ED mind. Yet as ED has become quieter, I have space now to dream again. This dreaming feels overwhelming.

It's as if I am staring at a map in which there are no routes, no trails—just a wide open landscape. At times the view from here is inviting, but I'm used to pre-built routes. Learning to build my own is scary. I want to cling to recreating others' paths—asking them how they got to where they are today. What left turn should I avoid? What's the easiest route to the "best" destinations? But I'm slowly learning there are no secret fast-track routes to a promised land where everything will suddenly make sense.

I remind myself of the strength I have inside of me, of my own resilience. I am reminded I am no longer the sick seventeen-year-old girl I once was. I do have a whole life ahead of me, one of constant exploration of learning and unlearning, just like recovery.

I'm not meant to have it all figured out. None of us are. There are no easy answers. There is only authentic connection with me and other humans to continue to light the way of this lost twentysomething.

Enough

I am back among the mountains. It's a tipsy night in Fort Collins, Colorado. I am surrounded by my old friend, Emma, and new friends, Alexa and Sophie. We are sipping on beers outside at Odell Brewing Company in the summer heat. Alexa and I begin to talk about meaningful experiences. I have been fairly quiet about sharing all parts of me to these new friends.

I fear the past will repeat itself, and I will be too much, or I'll be seen only as the girl with an eating disorder. But the alcohol mixed with Alexa's vulnerability loosens me up, mentally and physically, and we connect. She opens up about losing her mom and about her tattoos. I am so intrigued by how meaningful the ink on her skin is. I am in awe of her strength and resilience, her ability to talk openly about grief, and how she has and continues to evolve.

"Would you ever get a tattoo? What experiences have impacted you?" she asks.

Alexa sits with an inviting smile and a sense of calmness. She has just explained her *Be Here Now* tattoo and why being present with grief has built resiliency in her to provide space to heal. I feel welcome and safe; I tell her about my journey with ED. I reflect on how this summer marks my five-year recovery. I give her an overview of it all: my hospital stays, choosing recovery, and finding self-love through movement again.

I tell her about yoga teacher training and traveling. I tell her how a week in Colorado last summer showed me how expansive my life can be as I continue to let go of ED. I also tell her that through this all, I continue to learn the lesson that I am enough . . . just as I am.

She pauses. "Enough. Do you think you would ever get a tattoo of that?"

I smile. "Yes. I have wanted to ever since my diagnosis. I think I'm ready now."

We look at each other and start laughing.

"Let's do it!"

Emma is talking with another friend, and we tap her shoulder to tell her about our plans.

"Wait a second. In twenty minutes, you have gone from almost strangers to now getting a tattoo?" she asks, with a mix of joy and confusion.

"Why not?" I respond.

Emma drives us down to Main Street where we find a tattoo shop. Slightly tipsy, we walk in, and I tell the tattoo artist what I want. He agrees and asks where I want it.

I do not hesitate. I know I want it on my waist—the literal center of my body that I've spent so many years picking at and checking.

"My waist . . . and in my own handwriting," I say.

I write out the word "enough" a few times, my hands a bit shaky. I tell myself it does not have to be perfect. "Enoughness," although not an actual word, is me reclaiming my own imperfect worthiness. It's my way of reminding myself of my wholeness. Enoughness is a word filled with unique meaning. On the third time, I write the version he will engrave on my skin.

I lie on the table as he begins to bleed the ink into my waist. The ink marks the permanence of my enoughness. Yet the ink is much more than words on skin.

It reminds me of my healing and existence—pure and whole, not constrained by accomplishments. Enoughness empowered by a new understanding that if all I do is breathe here today, that is worthy. Enoughness underscored by a turning path of letting go of conditions that "define" my worth and letting in feelings that remind me I am complete. I know this truth through my every breath, a constant reminder between my racing thoughts.

He finishes the tattoo as a few tears drip down my face, not from the pain of the tattoo, but from the pain of releasing so many years of questioning my enoughness.

2,000 Miles Away

I sit in my cubicle, my hands trembling with eager uncertainty. Today is the day I'm supposed to get the call, to find out if I will finally have an opportunity to leave Ohio and bet on myself. The clock ticks, and I cannot focus on what our greeting card strategy should be for Halloween 2020. I cannot analyze whether or not there are too many witches and if the success of the top-performing card is due to the sentimental copy or the gold foil finishing.

The clock strikes 2:30 p.m., and my phone is still quiet. My Outlook calendar buzzes with the reminder of my one-on-one with my current manager, Jacki. More than a manager, she is a friend and mentor. Jacki reminds me life is more than your work. She challenges me to think critically and supports me with all my big ideas. She also reminds me there is more life outside of the walls of American Greetings and Westlake, Ohio, where I have spent the majority of my life thus far.

We take our meeting in a closed meeting room. My dad had warned me to "keep quiet" about this new job adventure because I should "never show my cards." He told me I needed to "play the corporate game." However, I decide to tell Jacki about my interview and the call I'm waiting for today. Jacki is not angry. She reacts with encouragement. We immediately scrap any items on our agenda, and she asks me discovery questions: "What gets you excited about this new opportunity? How would you feel moving across the country? How can I support you?"

I'm astonished by her support. We talk about my dreams and the stirring in my heart to get out, expand, and take a chance. I share how I want to push past my comfort zone and the confining certainty that fills most of my days.

About fifteen minutes into our conversation, my phone rings with a Seattle area code, 206. My trembling hands shake even more. My breath catches in the back of my throat. This is it—a moment when everything before and everything after is completely changed in a single pivot. I answer the phone on the third ring, trying not to seem too eager or desperate.

"Hey Allyson, this is Justin from Zillow. How are you?"

"I'm good. How are you?"

"I'm doing well. I wanted to ask how you think the interview went?"

Oh no, my mind begins to race. This means I didn't get it. He's probably going to coach me on how to do better. I take a deep breath, attempting to remain calm, despite this dialogue feeling like a minefield. I fumble on my answer, tongue-twisted. "Hmm, I think it went well? There are definitely parts I think I could have done better. But I really liked the team and the conversations."

Silence follows. I open my mouth to continue, but then I hear his voice on the other end of the line.

"Well, good. Because everyone agrees. They loved you and want to offer you the final spot in the business operations rotational program."

Silence. My life is about to change forever. I know this so clearly.

"Wow! Thank you. I am so excited! Thank you." Dumbstruck, this is all I can say.

"That's great to hear. You can take some time to think about it and let me know. We are on a tight timeline with the program starting in two weeks, but we wanted to let you know as soon as possible because you were the top candidate across the board. When do you think you may make a decision?"

Without even hearing what the final salary is and despite my father's warning to never say yes to a job right away, I know I will accept. I don't need to know where I will live or what the stock options are. All I know is I need to go. I need to answer that inner fire that says, *Leave, fly, baby, fly.* So on the phone right there, I say, "Yes I'm in—I accept!"

I gallop out of the room, my face radiating with glee. I walk over to Jacki's cubicle, and as soon as she turns back to look at me, she knows.

"You got it, didn't you?"

"Yes! I'm moving to Seattle!" I exclaim, as tears of joy wash over my cheeks.

Jacki gives me the biggest hug and tells me how excited she is for me. She tells me to go home and celebrate.

Because the office is within a short walking distance I operate in, I walk home, through my backyard, and run into the house, seeing my mom in the kitchen. I jump up and down while screaming at the top of my lungs.

"Oh, Alz, I am so excited for you!" she exclaims, watching me run around our kitchen. I'm overtaken by euphoria. I'm shaking, crying, screaming, and laughing.

"I'm doing it, Mama. I did it! I got it! I'm moving 2,000 miles away. I got a job at Zillow! Mom! I am doing this."

She looks at me with the largest grin.

"Yes, Alz, you are. And I'm so proud of you."

It takes me another thirty minutes to finally calm down from this high. Once I relax, my mind starts to race. The questions creep back in. *How can I let go of my support system? Will I relapse if I go?*

I don't have time to contemplate if I will relapse or what I will do if I can't hug my mom when I'm anxious. It's time to go—to sort through everything, pack my clothes, my life, my mind, my memories.

I have two weeks to pack any belongings, go through my twenty-three years of stuff, flash through two decades of memories, run through every favorite route, sit and think by the lake, drive through the Metroparks one last time, and take a few final after-dinner walks with my parents.

I have two weeks to quit my job, where I've spent the past three years building community. I have two weeks to let go of Steve, a person I've spent almost three years with, as long distance isn't an option. I have two weeks to take a chance, pack my two suitcases, jump on a plane—and go!

It's time to go. I feel deep within that I'm ready to leap, ready to get uncomfortable. The next day my mom and I book our flights. I find an apartment building, begin packing, and start letting go—releasing any expectations for what the next year may look like; releasing Steve, a man who has been so deeply integral to my life for several years; releasing who I was, who I am, and opening up to all I may be.

It isn't only my hometown. My eating disorder has also kept my world small. Still, I will move to Seattle where I know only one other person and take my soul 2,000 miles away. And despite knowing this moment is integral to my journey, I don't know all that is yet to come.

The stirring in my soul says to *fly. Let go. You are strong. Trust yourself.*

Letters from Elliott Bay

On the day my mom and I fly in from Cleveland to Seattle, I walk Elliott Bay for the first time. When I see the expansive water and mountains surrounding its perimeter, I let out a breath. No matter what this new place will bring, I can look out at the water, hear the sounds of the waves kissing the shore, and be called home to the same sounds from my youth. Mama and I walk as we share memories and reflect on how far I have come, how our adventures from Columbus have now led us to a journey 2,000 miles across the country.

My mom finds a bench during my first few days at work and writes. She tells me her wishes for me and how proud she is. She shares that whenever I feel lonely, to come back to the bay, specifically this bench, to feel her love. So I do just that. The path soon becomes the backdrop to learning and discovering, processing and hurting, and loving and being. With the water and mountains by my side, I write. My mom is here in spirit.

November 2019

I've been absent for a while. I'm learning what it means to have a true relationship with the only permanent person in life: myself. I'm learning how to find joy in simple moments like exploring a bookstore on a rainy day in my new neighborhood. I'm starting to speak kindlier to myself as if I'm speaking to a dear friend. I'm learning to express my feelings and let myself actually feel my emotions, from uncontrollable sadness to pure bliss.

December 2019

I sit in a sense of calmness, an envelope of wholeness and rightness. Slowly, little by little, I pull back layers. I recognize my scars. I open my heart. And I let myself in. I allow my own needs to arise, all those desires I've been shoving down for so long.

I've longed for so many years to have an authentic relationship. I didn't yet know who or what I was craving as I let bits of myself shine through. I realize the relationship I have been craving for so long is not with someone or something. It's with me. It's this honest dialogue with myself. It's a conversation in which I honor my truth. I tell myself to get quiet for long enough to hear all of it. These moments are not for anyone else but me. To fall apart. To come together. To shine.

March 2020 (One Week pre-COVID)

I sit here. A bench. Elliot Bay.

Although I feel so alone, I know I'm doing it. I'm learning how to heal my own heart. I'm learning what brings me joy and what steals my energy. I'm learning to take that chance to show up to a new group and try out a new hobby. I'm learning my feelings are fleeting, and that helps me embrace them. I'm learning to create my own joy. I'm learning to make myself laugh. I'm even learning to fall in love with who I am. All that I am.

ADAPT

During my second week at Zillow, I hear about the company's affinity networks that support underrepresented populations—Women's Network, Black Network, Latinos Unidos, PRIDE Network, and Asian Pacific Islander Network. At American Greetings, we had a group called the Young Professional Network for those under thirty. Ironically, at Zillow, most employees are under thirty. They have a group called ZG over forty. Then I hear of another group at Zillow, ADAPT, and it forces me to pause. I have never heard of a group that is created directly for those with disabilities. ADAPT stands for Able and Differing Abilities Partnering Together. It represents all who have a disability, both visible and invisible, and their allies. I am curious.

I connect over Slack with the ADAPT site lead, Kate, and she agrees to meet at the coffee tables on floor thirty-six of the Zillow Tower overlooking Puget Sound.

"Can you tell me more about what ADAPT is?" I ask. "I've heard it's for disabilities, but I would love to learn more."

Kate dives into her experience with ADAPT and all it encompasses. I hold back tears, as I have never felt so seen at a workplace before. There has always been this sense of "work Allyson" versus "Allyson." So much of myself is silenced in fear that it isn't appropriate to bring my full self to work.

As Kate begins to explain all that ADAPT is, I get full-body chills. My mind flashes through so many times I have created two versions of myself, and now here I am in a brand new place, 2000 miles away, and I am invited, even celebrated. Our thirty-minute chat turns into an hour-long conversation about both of our stories, the community of ADAPT, vulnerability, and how our stories make us stronger. Instantly, I know I belong.

Every two weeks, members of ADAPT meet for an hour-long coffee chat where everything said stays there, and what is learned leaves there. I'm surrounded by authentic humans who openly share how they're feeling—not a masked-up version, but the real deal. We all take turns sharing, *Here I am in my uncertainty, struggle, and resiliency.*

ADAPT is a home where people don't see my struggles as hidden puzzle pieces. They see my experiences as pieces of the puzzle that connect to one another, that are instrumental to who I am. With ADAPT, I eventually have the ability and honor to lead the community as president and learn every day about what it means to live in my own power. With ADAPT, I am welcomed with the opportunity to share my mental health journey on a large scale for the first time. My hands shake, and my heart races, as old shame voices bubble up. I take a deep breath and remind myself that to see change, I need to be a part of the change.

I look back at my seventeen-year-old self, depleted, defeated, scared as hell, wondering, "Why do I have an eating disorder?" I wish I could go back and tell her that one day what she thought would defeat her would become her superpower, that the process will show her why mental health is so important, and that each step is a part of a never-ending journey filled with peaks and valleys and everything in between. Her experience will lead her to pause and ask these continuous questions in a group where everyone celebrates their unique superpowers:

- What if instead of creating spaces of shame and stigma, we create spaces of bravery and vulnerability?
- What would it look like if instead of robotically saying "I'm fine" when asked how we are, we answer authentically and openly or, even better, ask each other, "How is your heart?"

- What if instead of looking at our differing abilities as weaknesses or parts we have to hide, we shift our lens and view them as our superpowers?
- What would it look like and feel like to be able to show up authentically, fully as we are?

Marathon of Self-love

"You will never be able to run a marathon. You have stressed your heart too much, and it will never be strong enough to run again. You will also likely relapse if you run long distance again. Your life will likely be confined to "easy" movement—yoga and walks. You will not be able to do strenuous exercise. You have damaged your body for good."

They handed me that verdict when I was seventeen years old in a hospital bed.

My chest feels unbearably heavy, not because of the weakness of my heart, but because of the thought I have damaged my body so much so that my life will never be the same. I can't breathe, not because of my feet pounding the pavement with adrenaline filling my lungs, but because I will never feel that feeling again.

They told me it wasn't possible. I refused to let them take the stars from my sky. *One day I will run again. I will be strong enough to feel the beating of my heart. I will prove them wrong. I will move my body for pure self-love, not hatred. One day I will cross a finish line that is not defined by how thin I am, but by celebration, compassion, acceptance, and love.*

Emma, an inspiring dreamer, motivator, connector, and friend came up with an idea she called the Purple Lace Project. She envisioned connecting communities to goals through sets of purple laces. I join this project 2,000 miles away from home on a walk along Elliot Bay. At first my mind says to run a half-marathon or hike a few mountains. But then I hear the North Star that pulls at the core of my galaxy softly say I can do more. I can run a marathon. So I write on the card Emma sent with my pair of purple laces: "To run a marathon as an act of self-love, embracing the journey along the way and pushing past my mental barriers."

Even writing the words gives me palpable, tingling energy. Fear creeps in and tries to convince me one doctor's verdict six years ago is the ultimate truth. Yet my hope, determination, and resilience burn brighter than my fear. Each day I lace up my purple laces, greet Elliot Bay with a grateful hello, and move my body. The blackboard in my apartment reads, "Go crush a marathon." It's my daily reminder I am whole and strong and capable.

Not every day is joyful. In fact, it feels much like recovery, like weaving paths that move me forward some days and to the side and backward other days. There are challenges in my mind of what my body should look like to run this race—the idea of smallness slowly creeps in. It doesn't stay. When I look down at my purple laces, I remember my North Star: self-love. Run for self-love.

On many of the runs, I feel I will never be strong enough, yet here I am. With every step and every run, I work through my feelings of loneliness in a city of strangers. I'm aware of all the emotions that come with taking chances each day. I pay tribute to the younger me who knew intuitively how to run for joy. I am running for her.

The fall crisp air touches my skin as we line up at the starting line. Waiting to take off, I'm not filled with regret and self-hatred. I'm alive with palpable energy, tingling self-love, bravery, resiliency, and determination, ready to engage in authentic movement. Due to an injury from training, I haven't run for a full month prior to approaching this starting line. After taking time to heal with a physical therapist, I'm able to step on that starting line determined to finish, no matter what.

The starting gun goes off, and we begin. I start too fast, energy and adrenaline radiating through my entire body. The miles continue on, and so many moments flash through my mind—lying in a hospital bed, taking my life and recovery into my own hands, saying I want to live, moving 2,000 miles away, every daily moment in which I chose to continue to rise, the little girl who learned to love running with her dad by her side. I run for those moments; I run for her; I run step by step—self-love, self-love.

Crossing the finish line after 26.2 miles, I experience emotions that feel brand new. During that marathon, I experience some of the hardest moments of my life. Despite those difficulties, I ended up feeling like it's one of the most rewarding and invigorating things I've ever done. It feels greater than flying out of an airplane or falling in love for the first time. It's the purest form of self-love I have ever felt. Despite all odds, despite the doubt I would ever run again, despite the fact that at one moment there was doubt if I would even live, I run on. It's a declaration to myself that I am here. That is enough.

Retreating in Solitude

On one of my solo walks, I stop at a bookshop I have been meaning to explore. There's no set plan for the day. It's just time with me to explore this new home. Inside the bookstore, I'm instantly comforted, drawn in by the power of stories that live on thousands of pages, words by souls I have never met, but they give me permission to enter their existence for a while. I'm no longer lonely as I connect with these stories.

I settle in on a big, comfy couch to soak in the sounds around me. Sitting among the tattered books, I don't crave connection with others. A familiar desire to be validated by another feels irrelevant here. Instead, I am connecting with myself. And here in the bookstore, as my wet, damp coat envelopes my body, I feel at home. I am with myself and all the beautiful rawness that comes with this experience.

I'm reminded this exact moment is why I took the chance to leave and move 2,000 miles away. These are the moments my soul was craving—the simple pleasures that don't need to be posted for the rest of the world to see. These little moments where I'm becoming closer to myself, where I am letting my mind be quiet enough for me to think again, write again, *be* again. I don't have to do anything or be with anyone. I'm learning to love the rain and welcome the loneliness.

Easy Like a Sunday Morning

Waking up, my arms stretch gently above my head. My jaw is clenched. I release and take a deep breath. Here I am—alive, pleasantly alone. My curly hair is messy and tangled, like the thoughts in my mind. I get up slowly. *I need to move my body.* Waking up still means *move*. Nothing can be done until then.

I pause.

Why? Why do I need to move right now? The sky is still black. The world is silently asleep. I can wake up slowly.

I pause again, leaning into my curiosity.

What am I needing? I long for words that meet my eyes, inviting me into stories, to worlds that are not my own. There is so much to learn and glean from these lives outside of my own.

I want the sound of beautiful melodies to build emotions in my body. It happens sometimes with words, other times with beats. Music can transmit deep sensations through my veins. I want these feelings right here, right now. I want space and time to string words together, sometimes in a meticulously delicate manner and other times with no care at all. I need to examine everything in my mind. I want to feel empowered, sad, hopeful, deep, and loved through words on the page.

I seek movement, but it doesn't have to happen all at once, at the instant my alarm rings. I can pause long enough to defeat the white-knuckling habits that ruled my life for so long. I can ask what I am authentically seeking. I can revel in slow mornings. I can embrace the space as I wake slowly and let it become a little bit easy.

Becoming Myself

I look into the mirror at my own reflection, placing one hand over my heart and one on my belly. I feel my heartbeat alongside the rise and fall of my breath. I hear only the sound of my own exhale in my 500-square-foot Seattle apartment. I feel deep in my bones that I am slowly becoming more of whom I have longed to be and that I am growing less attached to ED leading my every move. I don't fold over in the mirror today. Instead, I smile back with compassion and pride. I take these moments to notice all the scars that have built up as a result of following ED's every command—the daily beatdown, the neglect of my body, the complete abandonment of who I am at my core.

I open Spotify and play "Rise Up" by Andra Day. I shift from side to side, letting the movements flow. I'm not good at dancing, but this doesn't matter. I let my body expand, express itself, and flow to the rhythm of the lyrics. *Rise up, rise like the day.* I rise again and again, healing and becoming.

I embrace my body in a warm hug and cry. A soft *thank you* seeps into my mind. I move my fingertips across my skin. It feels strange at first, like I'm not allowed to experience this empathetic touch. I usually only allow myself to pick at my skin and feel disgust. This morning I crave to know the intricacies of my own body that carries me through life. I let my fingers float down my arms until they land again, one hand on my heart and one on my belly. The song ends, and I stand, head tall and feet grounded. For a moment I don't recognize the woman looking back at me. She is beautiful and worthy. I smile and remember: She is me. She's been ready for me to see I am becoming her.

Shutdown Marathons

The streets are quite silent compared to the masses of crowds that usually flood a marathon race. The pre-race jitters mirror the quiet around me. Instead of feeling competitive, full of desire to pass the person in front of me, I feel a sense of peace inside me. I'm not running for a certain time or to beat anyone. I'm here to put one step in front of the other. Today I thought I would be in Vancouver running a marathon. Instead, I'm here alone in the empty COVID world. I lace up my shoes and embark on a 26.2-mile solo journey, my race against me.

I am used to the masses of crowds, the streets closed, and the entire city knowing I am in the race. This time the city and the world are already shut down. People are tucked away inside their homes. My mind, my body, and I take one step at a time. My legs start off a bit heavy, and I begin to think I can't do this. The doubt slowly creeps in, yet slowly a small whisper says, "You've been here before." Then I take in a breath of remembering—my body knows, my mind knows—I've got this.

At mile twelve, the doubt creeps up again. My feet maintain their rhythm. But again, it's as if my body reminds me, *You've got this.* Then I hear, *Trust and let go.* I surrender to all the uncertainty, the fear, and the unknown. I let go. And then my body takes over, and my heart is filled with joy when I see friends and family cheering me on along the way.

My community of people form their own cheer squad as they ring cowbells, obnoxiously honk their car horns, and blast Kelly Clarkson's "What Doesn't Kill You Makes You Stronger" from their cars. I am greeted by kind strangers' smiles who ask what I'm doing as I casually

yell back, "I'm running a marathon!" This results in even more support to keep going. My grandma greets me with her homemade fin-
isher certificate at the "finish line." Through every step, every cheer,
every friendly hello, every cowbell, I am reminded of all the good in
this world. I thank my body for carrying me through from sickness to
strength. Most importantly, I am grateful for a community that cheers
me on every step of the way.

Sunrise Swims

The world is still closed, but each morning our community gathers right before the sky is lit up. An expansive body of water welcomes our bodies like a homecoming. The moment my body kisses the water's skin, I am filled with belonging, as if in the company of a familiar friend. We swim under the moon, not yet greeted by the sun. Stroke by stroke, the sun greets us with warmth and jubilant hues. We continue to float into the sun, our bodies moving as one with the water.

We swim here together each morning, and every time, I feel the strength in my body with each stroke, my back muscles pulling me through the water. My mind stills at the touch of water. We swim for a few miles each humid summer morning, testing what we are capable of and reveling in our ability to move.

During one of our morning swims, my teammate Mayra shares her sadness. Every year she typically participates in a six-mile big swim to honor her brother who passed away from cancer. However, due to COVID, they've canceled this event. I'm moved by her story, and I wonder how I can support her. We brainstorm what our version of this event could be. As a group, we decide to embark on our own big swim, like I did with my marathon.

I decide to swim from one end of Cleveland to the other, a ten-mile trek. I know the power of my mind and what I've overcome. I know I can swim for something bigger than myself and call on that strength when the waters get rough.

On a Saturday morning, I begin my ten-mile trek from one end of Cleveland to the other. The water is my home for the next five hours—challenging me, pushing me, calming me, moving with me.

At times it feels effortless, as if I belong nowhere else but in these waters. At other times, I doubt whether I can continue on for another stroke. My breath begins to calm as I count my strokes to the rhythm of my beating heart. My uncle kayaks next to me. I'm aware of his presence, but I don't touch the kayak, as I want to keep this swim "official." I wasn't trying to break any records, but I had my own personal goal, swimming all ten miles without touching any concrete objects.

I swim in honor of those who can't. I swim for the young girl inside me who loved to be in water and for Dr. Steve, Steve's father, who lost his battle to ALS. Every time I find myself in doubt, I come back to, *Remember your why.* I remember being a little girl with her worries about the way her belly looked in a bathing suit but could escape this angst in the water. I remember Dr. Steve, who despite the pain and suffering that accompanies ALS, smiled through it all.

As I swim, I think about my journey over the past seven years. All of it feels like the water this morning. It is filled with so much movement, no clear path, yet it invites a push to continue moving forward. During so many points across the lake, I want to stop. I reach a moment where I don't know if I can continue. Then I look down at my arm and see "Swim for Steve" inked on my skin with a permanent marker. Instantly I feel his joy radiating out through the sunshine. I decide I'm going to finish, no matter what.

Toward the end, I catch glimpses of land, of safety, of rest. I am fortunate enough to get to shore, which not all do. The trek has reminded me how capable I am, and that despite the rocky waters, I can carry on. One stroke at a time, I am welcomed home just as the water welcomes home the sun each morning.

There's something magical about being in the water. It wraps around my body like a liquid blanket of love, bliss carrying me along through the tide. The water reminds me everything is fluid; I can change directions at any moment, and there will still be support to carry me along. It teaches me bodies are beautiful, strong, majestic, and made for movement and connection. I dance among the waves. I am calm in the breaths between each stroke. The water welcomes me as I am.

Fluidity

I have dreamed of living in Colorado near the never-ending mountains for the past two years. I have dreamed of feeling expansive on the trails. I'm finally here, but I do not feel expansive. I feel lost and lonely. I have let go of Steve for the final time after trying again and again and again.

I wake up and go back to bed in my new home in Denver. I wish my heart would stop. I grab a journal to process my feelings, hoping I will look back at the strength and resilience I've demonstrated over the years. I feel like I should be over ED by now, but here I am again stuck in a cycle, questioning how I can continue on. The isolation hurts. I miss being surrounded by humans and laughter.

I am reminded again of how important it is to my recovery and my overall well-being to be around my community. The self-isolation makes it easy to go back to ED. I don't want to reach out. I feel like a failure if I admit again that I'm not okay. I wish someone else would reach out.

My friends sometimes check in. I fake a smile and tell them, "I'm fine." But deep inside, a storm is building, waiting to rage. I feel confused. They say time heals all wounds, but I feel so alone, unsure if time can ever heal the pain of ED.

A few weeks pass, and the pain persists. Someone asks me what I want to do with my future. All I can manage to tell them is "I don't know." Thinking about tomorrow is daunting. I can't even imagine thinking about what may be beyond that. I long to be empty again. I think the simplicity of that old emptiness will solve all my problems. Even seven years later, when I am in despair, ED grabs hold of me quickly.

Underneath it all, I know I'm still a few steps ahead of where I've been each time before. I know this healing is fluid. Although I feel at a new low, I'm not a failure. So I take action. I pick up my phone and call a hotline for the first time. It feels easier telling a stranger who doesn't know how long I've been dealing with ED, who won't judge that I'm here again.

The voice on the other side of the line asks me what I can do to carry on. I say I don't know. *No, I don't have a plan to kill myself. I don't have any plans at all. I don't know what the future holds. I do know that amid this fluid healing, I don't want to feel this empty.*

I agree I will try therapy again. I agree I will reach out to one friend. I agree I will try to carry on, even feeling the hopelessness. I will try to inhale and exhale, one breath at a time.

Icing

Most nights before I fall asleep, I say a prayer. I don't pray for good health or for my family. I don't pray for love or wealth or whatever else others may pray to some higher power about. I pray that in the morning I won't be awake; that the Higher Power could stop my heart while I am sleeping; that I could end it all, so I would never feel this pain anymore.

When I start my therapy sessions with Megan, I don't tell her about these prayers. I don't say I am well. I tell her I'm struggling, and I don't know if I want to continue to live. I also tell her I need a therapist who is direct. After seven years of on-and-off therapy, I know myself too well. I know I can easily smile, put on my mask, and tell you what I think you want to hear. I tell her that if she isn't willing to call me out on my bull-shit, then it won't work. I also tell her this time I want to talk about more than just my eating disorder. I assure her I recognize my eating disorder is an important part of my history, but it's not the only part of me.

This pain is much deeper than the eating disorder. I need someone to see beyond my eating disorder, force me to pull back the layers, get into the dirt with me, and dig into places that have not been touched in years.

After telling her my expectations, Megan agrees to work with me. She is not taken back by my assertiveness. Instead, she says she's proud of how I set a boundary and asked for what I needed during this time when my entire being calls for me to disappear.

It's our third session, and Megan starts our time together with these questions.

"What do you like about yourself? What makes you proud?"

I don't know how to answer her. I feel I'm nothing behind my job title, my one A– on my lifetime report card, my extreme work ethic, my race PRs, my yoga teaching certification, my friendships, my relationship titles—my list of various accomplishments.

"I guess I'm a good worker, and I'm a good runner. I guess I'm proud of myself for being a good friend, but I don't really have anything to be proud of right now. I have been in Colorado for a few months, and despite being physically healthier, I'm mentally lost. I feel depleted and hopeless. It seems as if I am trying to let go of ED and how I used to validate my worth, but if I do that, I'm unsure about what's left."

"I hear you," she says, nodding her head. "What I'm hearing is a list of accomplishments and accolades. But I'm not sure that's who you, Allyson, truly are."

I stare back, unsure how to respond.

"Can I offer something?"

"Sure."

"So there's this analogy I'd like to try with you. What you've just described is what I like to call icing. You have all these things you do, all these accomplishments and titles, but if all of that is stripped away, if there is no icing, who are you?"

Her words feel like a head-on punch to the gut. I feel completely wrecked.

"I . . . don't know."

Her eyes stare back at me with a deep empathetic understanding and a slight curve of her lips as if to say, *I know you don't know and that's okay. That's why I'm here.*

I'm sobbing now. She continues.

"And I also know that your cake is incredible, strong, and dynamic. And my hope for you is that we will uncover that cake and build on that together. So even when all the icing seems to be removed, you will still be Allyson because your cake is full and whole."

In my gut I can feel a certainty of truth through her words, but I don't know how to respond.

"I do wonder," Megan says, "why do you feel the icing—the accomplishments you just described—are so integral to your identity?"

It takes me a moment before the memories start spilling out.

"Well . . . when I was in first grade, our teacher asked us to write a one-page essay about who we are, and I wrote a twenty-four-page essay. In second grade, I set the school record for boys and girls for the most sit-ups in the physical fitness test. In third grade, I was selected to be in the high school play, even though they only usually accepted fourth graders."

She asks, "And why did you feel the need to do that? What were some of the messages you received from others as you accomplished those things?"

"Well, it seemed growing up that everyone told me I was destined for greatness. I mean, my teachers told me to remember them when I was a famous actress. I also think I put extreme pressure on myself. I felt if I was not exceptional, then I was nothing. I thought life was basically meaningless if I wasn't doing something extraordinary."

She nods. "And how do you think that impacted your eating disorder?"

My breath catches. I freeze. My entire world stops, as the pieces begin to fall into place.

"Oh my gosh" is all I can manage to get out before tears fall. Megan sits there with me, and I can feel her compassion wrap itself around me.

"My eating disorder is my icing. It's just another way for me to feel exceptional. When I was in the depths of my eating disorder, I was always the smallest one in the room, and I could set myself apart. It's just a way for me to finally be the most exceptional—I could outwork anyone at the gym and could have the best self-control. And then after starting recovery, I began to want to be exceptional at recovery."

Megan nods with a slight smile. "I think you may have just really hit on something deep. How do you feel?"

"I feel everything and nothing. Like my world finally makes sense. But I also feel empty because I have no clue who the fuck I am without my icing."

"That's what we will explore together."

So we do. We scrape away the icing, little pieces at a time, and build my cake. My prayers slowly change. I stop praying I won't wake up the next day. Instead of saying that every night, I only occasionally asked for that to happen. After a while, I no longer pray for it at all. Slowly the triggers that sparked my ED become more manageable. And slowly I begin to understand what is under my icing.

Letters from the Trails

I'm in a pandemic, and I'm trying to do anything to feel alive. I'm trying to find out who I am beyond my icing. I do what I know how to do. I walk new mountain trails. I let myself feel and I write again and again. These are letters from those days—my chronicle of hurting, healing, moving, and expanding as I know how.

January 2021

I walk among the trails, the dirt, and me. I don't know which way I am headed on the trail. I just walk. It feels quite synonymous to how I feel in life. This map feels brand new and unclear. I try to let curiosity guide my way as I follow the natural curves of the trail. I let out deep bellowing cries, feeling the grief of letting go of someone who has been my person for five years. The food is the hardest part. Each time I eat, I think of Steve, as he showed me how beautiful and healing food can be. I wonder what an ending without him looks like. I don't know. I do know I can move one foot at a time, leaning into the unknown.

February 2021

I continue to walk a new trail every weekend. I continue to explore. I continue to let go. In this letting go, the voices begin to shift. At first, they told me I need to know it all. Now they say, *Throw your plans to the wind, let the sounds of the earth be your guide, and trust your feelings.* I feel the weight of my backpack grow lighter as I emotionally let go. I've been holding onto so much pressure for so long—wanting to be perfect, thin, fit through doors, approved, exceptional. All this pressure is overwhelming. I recognize how hard I've always been on myself and invite compassion in. It's okay to not know. It's okay to just move freely. It's okay to let go.

April 2021

I'm learning a new language that feels foreign to my soul. I don't always search for the hardest hike or the tallest peak. I walk along a level terrain that brings calmness to my body. I feel most peaceful when I'm full of stillness on top of the mountain. In this quiet and expansive space, I'm reminded I'm not a human doing; I'm a human being. No matter how many trails I climb, I'm me.

Here I Begin

My entire body is in a full sweat, and my breath feels as rapid as my racing heart. I wake up in shock that I am alive. I've just dreamed I was about to jump. It feels as if I'm in a constant struggle to understand who I am. Who am I without a number of miles to determine my worth? Who am I if my job title is stripped away? Who am I without my near 4.0 GPA? Who am I if my body is no longer the smallest in the room? I contemplate these questions each day and wonder why I should carry on.

In this dream, I'm standing on a cliff, surrounded by water. Different people walk in and out of my view. Some are familiar, like Steve and my mom. Some are strangers. I stand at the edge and contemplate jumping off. I wonder if I jump, if I can swim in the beauty of the water forever. After that thought, a hand reaches into the frame and takes me off the cliff. I step away from the edge, crying, my breath uneasy. When I wake up from the dream, there are dried tears on my cheeks, and my breath is heavy. I wake up with different thoughts than when I went to sleep.

"I don't want to leave this place yet. I want to be here to embrace all there is to explore. Here, I begin."

At Home with Strong Women

A home is just a structure if it's not filled with support, love, and connection. Throughout my journey, my home has been built and rebuilt brick by brick. Each person I've encountered has helped me build this home. When I think of what continues to build my strong foundation, I think of my women—all who support me, inspire me, empower me, and remind me who I am and all I am meant to be. The women I reflect on below are only a snippet of the multitude of impactful women who fill my home. As I continue to move through life, I know each woman I meet will add to my home and my garden as we connect and flourish together.

Evelyn, My Foundation

The foundation of my home is rooted in a woman named Evelyn. On the corner of Indianpath and Laughlin Lane, I met a hazel-eyed, slightly quiet, four-year-old named Evie. At the time, I did not think this kid would be my friend. In our elementary school days, we were set up to be frenemies. Growing up, we both had an extreme desire to succeed, and instead of seeing this as a beautiful way to grow and push one another together, we saw it as a playing field in which only one could win.

However, as we got older, we saw our drive and ambition were not meant to tear each other down but to build each other up. When we embraced the notion there was more than enough room for both of us in this world, we flourished as a team. Through our past competition, we shared an in-depth understanding of each other—our strengths and our areas for opportunity. At this time in our lives, we could celebrate each other's authenticity. There is something so special about having someone in your life who knows you that well.

Evelyn was there for me at my lowest points and sat with me on the Westlake Rec Center hill after leaving the hospital the first time. "I'm so proud of you. I'm glad to have you back. I've missed you."

In high school and college, we talked as we walked in the Cleveland Metroparks. On those trails, we told stories of first heartbreak and our doubts that we would ever heal. We shared our fears of being too much and our worries we would never feel like we are enough. Together, we experienced the wonder of finding peace in our pasts as we broke through the cobwebs in our minds.

When I left for Seattle and then to Colorado, Evelyn was no longer a Metropark walk away. Instead, we talked on the phone while we walked our separate paths around our new homes. Despite the distance, hearing her voice always felt like home.

We leave each other reminders that it's okay not to be okay. I often return to her saved voicemails when she tells me I don't need to do this life alone. She says, "Hey, it's me, a little teary-eyed, and I just thought I would check in on you. I know you're having a rough day, and I just wanted to say I love you, and you're incredible and life sucks sometimes, but we're gonna get through it."

With our twenty-two years of friendship, Evelyn is undeniably my foundation. This isn't just because we've known each other through so many seasons of life; it's how we approach life with each other. Evelyn sees my soul for what it is. She has held me at my lowest, wondering if I could carry on, celebrated me at my highest, and has loved me unconditionally in between. Evelyn shouts my praises from mountaintops when I silently fear falling off the top. She calls me out on potentially harmful behaviors and still loves me through it all. She reminds me we all need support. We need others to carry us through the tides when the waves feel too big to ride on our own.

Ashley, My Windows

"Hey, do you wanna go out with us?" Ashley asks.

It's my second semester of sophomore year, and I haven't been out all semester. Consumed again by the need for routine and smallness, I'm very hesitant to go. A small knowing inside of me says *go*. So I do, and the night sparks a friendship that brightens my life. We dance on tables, and Ashley makes me laugh more than I have laughed in ages. Ashley has a natural sense about her to make everyone feel easy and light. Like open windows on a partly cloudy day, she is the sunlight that peeks in at the perfect time. Ashley is my sunlight.

After a particularly hard day during senior year, Ashley fires a round of sarcastic jokes, and we blast music, dancing on top of our coffee room table. I instantly forget about the day, and I am filled with light. As we have grown older, our phone calls often consist of laughing until our bellies hurts, making light of the hardships of life. She has been there for me when I've needed to let go of different loves and navigate the ups and downs of recovery. Through it all, she manages to make me laugh despite the tears. She embraces my spirit of adventure, always joking, "So which continent are you on now?" Around Ashley, I let down my walls and let in joy.

She shows me that no matter how dark life can seem, we can always find windows of light.

Janki, My Door

When I met Janki during my junior year at Ohio State, it felt as if I was reconnecting with an old soul from a prior life. She challenges me to think big and question what it means to live equitably. She does this with such grace and compassion that I find myself constantly wanting to dive deeper and explore how I treat others. Janki shows me newness isn't scary. It's exciting. She is my door to inviting in possibilities.

The way she moves through life, Janki demonstrates that possibility is not held in one way of being but by letting yourself be open to a multitude of doors. Janki struts through the streets of New York City like a goddamn queen, dancing along the way. Her laughter is contagious and fills my belly with pure bliss.

When I wondered if I could actually take the job in Seattle, Janki was my first call. She had zero doubts. She showed me what was possible. "Ally, you're going to crush it out there. You're smarter than you think, and I know you can do this!"

She builds an equitable community in which each person in her presence has an equal seat at the table. She shows me I don't need to wait around for anyone to open my door. I am more than capable of going wherever I want. She tells me I'm a gift and I belong. When I feel lost and afraid of what may come, Janki makes me instantly know I can open any door unapologetically, just as I am.

Kelly, My Walls

When I first met Kelly at Ohio State, she radiated the purest form of authentic joy. We met at a table during sorority rush, and Kelly made me feel genuinely welcome. I knew we had to be friends. Kelly can reflect back to me the truest version of myself. She sees the world from a lens of pure beauty, assuming the best intent always. She makes me question what is truly important in this world. Kelly shows me the purest form of living is built on vulnerable connection.

Kelly builds her own walls, filled with individuality. She sees the world through a lens that captures the simplest moments of the rawest forms of beauty—both through her eyes and through the lens of her camera she uses to document her life's adventures.

On a cold January night in Seattle, I felt so alone and exhausted, unsure how long the grayness of the bleak sky would carry on in my heart. In that time of trouble, Kelly showed up for me with my favorite jar of almond butter and the sweetest smile. She wrapped me in her walls of comfort.

Kelly shows me that no matter how many miles away I am, I can listen with unconditional understanding. She shows me we are the builders of our own walls, worthy, no matter what.

Emma, My Roof

Emma has a natural ability to see the world as much more than a place where we just exist. She is constantly pursuing whatever makes her feel free. She lets her mind take her to unchartered waters and trails. She leans into her discomfort. She lives an unconventional life. She continually shows me there is no limit to how high our roofs can be.

Emma craves adventure and pushes me to get uncomfortable. After spending an hour with Emma, I'm inspired to climb a mountain, read a new book, try skiing for the first time, take on my passion project, and change the damn world! I can feel the flames in her delicately fierce movement in each step she takes. Emma thrives on seeing humans connect and bringing stories to life. She started a Purple Lace Project to empower women to pursue goals that pushed them outside their comfort zones.

With Emma, I dared to get a tattoo, climbed a 100-foot rock, hiked fourteeners, planned business proposals, questioned the meaning of life, cried deeply and fully, and felt so fully empowered and loved. When my mind is spinning with ideas, and curiosity is running through my veins, Emma is the ignitor to set the ideas into motion. Emma is a dreamer, a doer, a lover. Emma cheers me on when I am at my highest of highs, when inspiration flows. She also walks hand in hand with me when my dreams feel nonexistent, when I question if I can carry on to the next morning. She stands in her truth and empowers those around her to do the same. She sees me for who I am and loves me fully and deeply. She believes in me and sees me in all my potential. Emma pushes me to limits I didn't even know I could reach. She instantly makes me remember how fully capable I am and encourages me to continue growing my roof taller than I could ever imagine.

Letters to My Younger Self

Letter to my Twelve-Year-Old Self
(from my Twenty-Two-Year-Old Self)

If I could tell my twelve-year-old self something, I'd tell her she's smart and kind and strong and loving. I'd tell her she's beautiful, and her beauty doesn't define her. I'd tell her that her mind is just as beautiful, if not more beautiful, than her body. I'd tell her that her body is hers, and she has the power and control to do what she chooses with it. I'd tell her one day she will find a man who will show her physical touch can feel like love and will electrify her soul all the way to the tips of her fingers and toes. I'd tell her one day she will break down crying in the middle of a yoga class during teacher training and place her hands on her belly, shaking while telling her belly, "I love you."

Although I can't tell her those things, I know now, ten years later, all of this has helped to shape me into who I am today.

I deserve to feel love and honor. I deserve to respect my body and expect respect from those around me. I deserve to explore what physical touch means for me in all of its forms, not just sexually.

I know through this all, I still am enough. I know I will use these lessons to remind young girls in this world that they, too, are enough and deserve to love themselves fully in their mind, body, and spirit.

Letter to my Seventeen-Year-Old Self
(from my Twenty-Four-Year-Old Self on
my Seven-Year Hospital Anniversary)

One day you'll be standing on a beach after a beautiful morning swim, and you will feel strong. One day you won't spend hours at war with yourself and your body. One day you'll eat sweet potato fries and chocolate peanut butter ice cream. The food will be delicious, and your belly and heart will be filled with joy. One day you'll know you are worthy of a life of joy.

You're so deeply loved. Speak kindly to your body because it will carry you on adventures you can't even imagine. Remember your mind and body are a team. Be kind to yourself. You only get one chance at this adventure-filled thing called life.

You Are My Sunshine

Mama's handwriting is tattooed on my skin as a forever reminder that she is always with me. Mama writes me notes wherever I go. She started writing these notes when I was a child. I'd find them in my brown lunch bags with simple permanent marker messages written on folded napkins. I never hid these messages from my friends at the lunch table, thinking I was too cool. Instead, I was excited, wondering what the note might say that day. Some notes included a simple joke. Other times I found a drawing of a simple cloud with a smile. My favorite notes included her hand-drawn sunshine with the words "You are my sunshine."

Mama writes me notes whenever I leave for a new adventure— college, a trip, leaving for a job 2,000 miles away, moving to Denver. Each year I left for college, she hid notes throughout all my packed items, twenty-one notes for my lucky number twenty-one. They were hidden inside books and in between packed sweatshirts. As I moved to Seattle and then Denver, she magically somehow included notes in each move. I find these notes at the most opportune times. It is often on the days I miss home and Mama most, or I'm having a bad day, that I stumble upon a note. Smiles, tears, Mama's warmth—I feel it all in these notes.

She reminds me often of the joy and zest I bring to this world. "You are like the sun," she tells me. "You truly make the world brighter." Mama is *my* sunshine, even on the darkest days.

Her words are now tattooed on my skin forever, reminding me always that she is with me. She is joy; she is bright; she is love. She shines like the sun, and so do I.

Hunger through a Baby's Eyes

I am twenty-six as I watch my five-month-old niece, Emma, squirming feverishly and crying. Her cries are her body's instinctive way of saying, "I need food." Her body thirsts for nutrients—to grow, to provide her with the fuel she needs. She is naturally hungry. Her hands reach out for the bottle as she cries. I watch her in awe. This five-month-old human knows. She knows her body needs these nutrients to carry on.

But as I watch my niece, I begin to wonder: *Are you sure you need that bottle? You're drinking it so fast; slow down. You may get too full. Are you sure you're really hungry?*

She continues to grab for the bottle, despite my silent worries. Why do I think my manipulated mind knows more than the untarnished instincts of a human body not yet corrupted by the world's ideals?

I notice these thoughts pass through my mind, and I answer my own question. I doubt her body's innate response because I have questioned mine for so long. She eats and eats and then pushes the bottle gently away when she is full. Another signal her body gives. She responds primally with her hands pushing away to say, "I am not hungry anymore." She knows; she listens; she trusts. Why don't I?

This small human shows me how deeply my body also knows. Fourteen years after I questioned my hunger for the first time, I still question it. I watch in awe; Emma doesn't have these doubts. She trusts, she cries, and she knows. What would it be like if I could listen to my hunger without question like my baby niece?

My Belly and Me

I feel the morning air breeze through the door of his room's balcony as the sun kisses my skin through the shades of the door. I'm entangled in the sheets with a man I'm in a new relationship with. He draws me to him and wraps his arms around my belly. He kisses my neck gently and whispers, "I love your tummy."

I don't know what to say. I have dreaded this part of myself for so long. I work over and over again to speak kindlier, pick a little less, and make peace with my belly. It's hard to accept that another human not only accepts this part of me, but he loves it.

I take a deep breath and rest my hand upon his as they both rest on my belly. I imagine one day my belly will carry life. Who will that be with? I don't know. I now know my belly is capable of this grand enterprise. I hadn't had a period for almost seven years. When I started menstruating again, and my period showed up for three months straight, I cried tears of relief. I am healing mentally and physically. And as I rest my hands on my belly, it's as if my belly whispers back, *Thank you.*

After hearing his words, I look up at him and hold his gaze for a moment. "Thank you," I say. "I do too." The "I do too" comes as a shock to my own ears. I am slowly starting to feel gratitude for my belly more often than hatred, but I still struggle to express this out loud.

And still, here I am, letting my body be open and vulnerable, letting my belly exist and be loved. I'm letting my entire being heal, knowing it can one day carry a child if I decide to go down that road. My belly and me, we are on the same team.

Wrapped in a Pretty Bow

Megan pauses. I am silent.

"Do you mind if I share something with you?" she asks.

Typically I'm the one sharing while she listens. As a therapist, she does most of the listening, and I do most of the talking. Megan is a different therapist, different from anyone I have ever met in my past seven years of therapy. She challenges me to go deeper than I ever have before.

"One thing I've noticed since we started working together is you've made a really authentic shift. It's not necessarily a bad thing, and it's something I often see as a strength, but it seems that every time you share something, there needs to be a resolution or a lesson. That often is great, but what I'm noticing lately is you don't need to find a resolution, and you're okay with letting whatever is just be. It's as if you no longer need everything to be wrapped in a pretty bow."

I'm no longer merely silent; I'm speechless. It's true. Lately I've become more comfortable with this idea of not needing to be okay, but as a writer I still try to find meaning in every experience. My way of processing is finding out why something is happening.

Yet here I am as Megan affirms that making sense of every situation, trying to wrap it all in a pretty bow is not always serving me. She tells me it's more than okay to feel the feelings and let that be enough; it's all right not to find a deeper meaning in every situation.

Pretty bows are pretty when they're pieced together. When they're taken apart, they're mere ribbons. The intricacies of the pretty bow lie in the work to craft the bow, not the outcome. The depth of the pretty bow lies in each of the threads used to weave the fabric together.

Now therapy sessions often end with, "So, that's how it is," or "So, that's what I've been feeling lately." I don't have to convey any meaning of life at the end. I just let myself be fully in it, seeing the threads of my bow.

Let Me Go

I have dated Shane for nine months now. Despite the deep physical intimacy, something doesn't feel right. He often makes me feel as if I'm too much. He questions my passions and their validity. As I continue to get healthier, my passions grow. I continue to try on a variety of things. I want to follow my curiosity, not succumb to a box of movement and food. For him, it's too much. Instead of trying to shrink myself to be enough in his eyes, I embrace the pain of letting him go. I want to expand; he wants me to be smaller.

I am reminded again and again of who I am. I tell myself whom I'm meant to be with will accept me fully. With this person, I will continue to learn to accept myself. Shane wants me to be quiet. To him, my loud voice is intimidating. I still speak boldly and with fire about all my passions. To him, it seems chaotic. To me, it's how I operate. I don't want to live this life doing one thing.

I recognize how I often used to doubt these parts of me, hide them, or even try to deplete them. But I feel most free when I'm not confined to finding that one thing, when I lean into what I'm feeling that day.

Shane says I'm all over the place with my passions. I see it as being curious. If I want to be a yoga teacher, work at a brewery, teach kids English, be an author, start a nonprofit, be a trail guide, learn to surf, jump off cliffs, that's not unfocused. It's blissful and unapologetically curious.

I recognize this is me. Shane and others may see it as too much, but I've spent time—over and over again—realizing and understanding I'm not too much. I'm bold, I'm whole, and I'm enough. I'm like water—constantly flowing, tides changing day by day. I can say with certainty I love who I am, and I'm not going to compromise that for anyone or anything. I know at my core, I'm none of these titles or jobs. I'm curious. I love deeply. I live wholeheartedly. And I will keep doing so.

I must stand in my truth and tell him to embrace it or let me go because it's time I refuse to let anyone shrink me. I will honor my truth. I'm allowed to be here, and I'll keep taking up space.

Dear ED

July 22, 2021

Hi ED,

It's been a while. You've been in my life for quite some time. I remember meeting you back in high school at Annie's gym. You crept in quietly at first and then head on, tumbling slowly at first, then viciously fast. When I felt out of control, worthless, empty—you were there. You helped me get through a lot—thank you. You also took away too damn much. You took away nights with friends, dancing, and eating ice cream; you took away my self-love. You stripped me of my laughter and my smile. You deprived me of my bubbly, full-of-life personality. You pushed me into a deep relationship in which you were the only person allowed—you turned the relationship into an obsession.

Slowly I've been creating distance from you. You moved from being a constant thought to only a phone call away, to someone I rarely call. I don't need you to be extraordinary. My laugh does that. I don't need you to be loved. I'm loved no matter what. I've wanted to bid you farewell for so long, but part of me really didn't want to release you.

I've felt so much freedom lately, and that's because I've started to really let you go. Damn—eight years in the making, and I'm finally ready to say goodbye. I know you may come lurking back from time to time knocking, but I'm not going to answer this time.

I know you told me I'd never be rid of you; I'd never have kids; I'd never have a life without you. Well, guess what? I can and I WILL live without you, AND I can have kids one day if I choose. And yes, I am HEALTHY without you.

It's time to part ways. You've held the power for way too long. The future without you is damn scary. I don't know what it will look like, but I'm ready to discover it because I know life without you is bound to be incredible. I've had small tastes of it so far, and I can't wait for all that is to come. Bye ED—thanks for teaching me resilience, empathy, and self-love. I love me without you.

The Ocean's Expanse

I am listening to Hawaii's waves on a month-long respite from my life in Denver. The past month has felt overwhelming. I'm again letting go of a person I cared for deeply. And in this release, I question my enoughness. But with the sun kissing my skin and the sound of the waves, my heart feels still. The noise in my head is quieter. I can take time to observe.

I notice as the waves crash in and out with force. As they move with speed and purpose, the ocean moves, flows, rises, and falls. Like the wave, I can stop listening to the refrain "I am too much." This time, I let this thought pass as I come back to the tide where I may be just right, not too much at all.

I look over the expansive sea, as I am inspired by her breath and depth and the fact that I can't see far enough to know what's on the other side. There is peace in this unknowing. At the thought of the wide-open surface, I'm reminded that I, too, deserve to expand, not just in a physical sense, but in the way I live and grow and learn.

I learn from the ocean's body as she never apologizes for taking up space. She is dynamic, her tides changing with the pull of the moon. She is vast, holding life within her depths. I close my eyes, and instead of breathing in "I am too much," I breathe in, "I am ready to expand." I breathe out. I blink my eyes open as I smile at the waves, thanking them for reminding me to live deep in high tides and low.

Broken Body

My body feels broken. The doctors were right. Maybe I am not supposed to move in the ways I crave to move. Seven years of no period, my body is finally saying I have had enough. It feels as if my body is against me. I sit inside the doctor's office reviewing my MRI scans.

"Your scans are a bit interesting. You do have a labral hip tear, which we expected. However, I think most of your pain is coming from two stress fractures and osteitis pubis. You have a stress fracture on your sacrum and on your lesser trochanter."

Hearing his words, part of me wants to laugh, and part of me wants to sob. I cannot believe this is happening again. This is my sixth stress fracture in a year. I don't understand why. I'm finally doing all the right things. I'm fueling my body, working with a running coach, doing my physical therapy exercises, resting as much as I can, and still, it seems my body is against me.

It feels as if she is providing payback for all the damage I put her through over the years. I walk out of the appointment and into my car. I can't drive. I'm engulfed with emotion, my body shaking as my hands grip the steering wheel. I let out a bellowing scream. *Why is this happening? Why couldn't I have just loved my body? Why is my body against me? When will I finally be ready to be on the same team?*

I don't know. I drive to Sloan's Lake and sit by the water as I let the water from my eyes pour out. *I am not broken*, she whispers. I hug my knees into my chest. *I am so sorry*, I whisper back.

I look onto the lake and remember I've been here before. Despite the brokenness, I know this time my body and I are united. I try to accept the truth. The truth is I can't change the past. I can't go back and stop my younger self from running her body into the ground. I can't go back and tell her it's not her versus me; it's us.

I can heal this time, for her. I can try to release the blame and invite in acceptance. I can also let myself feel broken and feel the pain of being here again. I know she didn't know any better. I will let myself release the pain, and I will forgive her. A small voice inside me whispers, *This is not my broken body. This is my healing body.*

Allowing Grief

My phone reminds me of a photo from eight years ago. I'm in Europe, desperately thin with a concave face. I sit in my Denver apartment bed and gaze at the cold nighttime sky. The only light comes from my phone. I wonder who that girl in the picture is. She seems like a ghost, a figment of who I once was. I look at her and see her pain, her desperate cry for help. But another part of me aches deeply to go back.

I know I was sick, but after so long, it's easy to romanticize this time. It feels as if I am letting go of a part of me that has been integral to how I cope, how I lived for a near decade. After all this time, I'm still afraid to cut the cord for good. What will my life truly be like if I fully let go? ED gave me drive, determination, and grit. Who can I be without this never-ending pressure to be the best?

At the time, I didn't have to question my worth. My "worth" was rooted in my thinness, my drive, my compliments from the gym. Now I'm forced to face this murky human condition without the comfort of thinness, trying to figure out what actually gives me worth.

I don't know exactly why, but I miss the days when my life was consumed by exercise. I didn't have to think about anything else because my mind was too consumed by my next workout. I didn't have to think about big life questions, which kept me small with a different kind of safety. Now that I actually have to deal with the fullness of life, I feel overwhelmed.

While I grieve letting go of my ghost, my body continues to whisper, *Please do not go back. Please let me stay here. Please don't try to change me. Don't try to move me beyond my bounds; love me here.*

I think of the reasons I love those dear to me. It has nothing to do with the shape of their bodies. My vessel is beautiful because it contains laughter and friendships and adventure; it contains a state of vitality and newness.

I look away from the picture and close my phone. I cry deeply for all that was. As I expand out from the image of what once was, I take in what is. I can let my body evolve and grow just as my life evolves and grows. She will always be a part of me. She is the reason I let myself grieve and expand all at once.

Leave Her Wild

I remind myself of what it was like when I was young, the feeling of being free and full and alive. I remind myself of the young girl inside of me who wants to roam effortlessly.

I remember summer nights running blissfully along Laughlin Lane. I think of climbing trees and cabinets, "like a monkey," Mama says. I think of the first time running with my dad, every ounce of my body electrified. I flash back to moments singing and acting on stage—immersed in the energy of the audience, while captivated by experiencing what it may be like to live in another's world. I think back to screaming from mountaintops and jumping into a Colorado glacier. I am flooded with snapshots of sips of coffee, sunrises, and sunsets, losing myself in books, hiking on trails, and living. In all of this, I yearn to feel. I long to be free, unconfined by any chains, fueled instead by wholeness and deep desires.

When my final bell tolls, I'll have traveled mountains and seas. I'll have watched life grow and blossom from the pit of my belly. I'll have danced through streets and sung from rooftops. I'll have known what it means to love fully and wholly, both myself and others. I'll have taken chances and risks. I'll have felt deep and full belly laughs. I'll have felt fear, and I will not be paralyzed by the feeling of fear. I'll move fully in my expansive body. Through mountains, across oceans, and everything in between, I'll have left her wild.

Beyond My Body

I spend two weeks in Hawaii. I swim next to a seal, and my days are bookended by the sun's rhythm. There is nothing to be measured. There is no scale of validation. There is no proof of worthiness. On this island, I feel so content and at peace, and I question why.

I had always thought that when I get to some abstract "there," then I'll be happy. Or if I have a certain job, then I'll be happy. Or when I have the perfect body, then I'll be happy. When I get to the thinnest version of me, then I'll be happy.

But I'm here with my feet in the sand, the water and sun all around, and I have none of that. And still, I'm happy, full, present, and alive. I have space to think and a wide-open world to explore.

I recognize I'm content because I finally understand my life begins beyond my body. I recognize, too, there is no finish line to cross. There are only moments entangled with one another, seemingly going nowhere, yet connected when I look closely. I know now there is truly no goal that will serve as my "ultimate" happiness. There is only here and now and people, places, and presence. There are simple moments and big moments and everything in between. Letting in a life beyond my body, I'm happy. And for now, that is enough.

Epilogue: I Am From . . .

I am from a beautiful blue-eyed soul and the hardest working man,
from unconditional love and empowerment and success.
I am from laughter on Laughlin lane,
from horse barns turned into mansions,
from nightly walks and freshly cut grass.
I am from Julie's house filled with animals,
to Clorox and dust pans (no pets allowed).
I am from a pink tethered blanket, comforting my busy hands.

I am from a blue Cinderella dress and pink sequin tutus,
from gold stars and loud, open mouths.
I am from characters on scripted pages and the star of the show.
I am from stages and shining lights,
from a ladybug in a peach and a Hollywood dream.
I am from black chained paints, and I am a thespian.
I am from freedom and escape.

I am from tied soccer cleats and elbows and yellow cards,
from you are not fast enough, B teams, and cupcakes.
I am from sweat and grit and persistence,
from I will make it, and you aren't good enough.
I am from horse and knockout,
from my father always letting me win one-on-one.
I am from jumping up to nets and sprints across courts,
from spikes and digs on the ball and on my heart.

I am from pink-striped shirts and Santa Claus bellies.
I am from thin is beautiful, and I am not thin enough.
I am from mischievous pictures sent to malicious eyes.
I am from I don't deserve to be seen, and I just want to be heard.
I am from toilet-paper-filled pools and words carved into wooden decks.
I am from words cut deep, and I am not worthy.

I am from your worth is held between a boy's hands,
and you are an object for his benefit.
I am from beauty is success, and your smile is money.
I am from prematurely large breasts touched too soon,
from broken hearts and empty promises.
I am from your body is for others' use.
I am from plastered-on smiles, and you are not enough.
I am from fast crowds and drunken nights,
from class president and goody two-shoes.

I am from perfection and worth defined by grades,
from numbers on scales and numbers on a machine.
I am from StairMasters and demons in my mind,
from calorie trackers and seventeen-day fix diets.
I am from you will never get rid of me,
and its grip is too strong.
I am from I can't stop, and I have no control.
I am from I do not need anyone except anorexia.
I am from lost friends and lost self.

I am from a hospital bed and a week left to live,
from I have beaten this, and recovery is not linear.
I am from a second hospital stay and a semester off college.
I am from I will beat this, and I can do this.
I am from a powerful support system and selflessness.
I am from my smile is a gift, and my beauty does not define me.

I am from I can make an impact, and I will change others' lives.
I am from empowerment and love.

I am from rubber mats and deep breaths,
from vinyasa and tadasana and the power of mindful movement.
I am from leaving people in their greatness
and authentic human connection.
I am from loving hands on my belly,
from a place of wholeness and completeness.
I am from I am enough. I am enough. I am enough.

Acknowledgments

I am still in awe that I'm even writing an acknowledgments page right now. Writing this book has been one of the most rewarding, healing, and truly soul-opening experiences of my life. And none of these experiences, nor the words on these pages, would be possible without the village of people who have touched every part of my journey, especially **my immediate family**.

To Mama Suz, I truly would not be here without you (literally and figuratively). From holding me as I cried, to refeeding me, to being my biggest cheerleader, to reminding me every day of my resilience and joy, you truly are my sunshine.

To my greatest hero, Daddy, thank you for always reminding me of my worth and teaching me laughter is the best medicine. Thank you for showing me the power of running and movement.

To Sissy, thank you for buying me the journal in the hospital that started this all and for loving me with so much grace.

I am eternally grateful for **every woman** who has shown me uniquely what it means to take up space and embrace who you are. I could have included so many women here, but I want to specifically thank a few.

To Lauren, my first best friend, thank you for your words on July 23, 2013. While at the time I didn't want to hear those words, I now know you said them out of the deepest love and care. You saw in me what I couldn't see.

To Ev, I will forever cherish our Metropark walks and embracing the messiness of life one step at a time.

To Emma, thank you for showing me how expansive life can be—that we can chase our dreams, and we are worthy of the view from the highest mountaintops.

To Kelly, thank you for always holding space and empowering me to listen to understand, not to respond. Thank you for our adventures in Seattle and creating space for me to heal.

To Janki, thank you for being my dancing queen, life chaser, and embracer of childlike wonder. You empower me to never lose my zest for life.

To Ashley, I am forever grateful for the pure joy and laughter you add to my life, for walking each step of this journey together, albeit far in distance but never apart.

To Madi, thank you for empowering me every day to stand up for what I deserve, to speak my truth, and to never let anyone dull my sparkle.

To Allegra, you know my soul at times as if we shared the same parts. Thank you for showing me I am worthy of a life that is full and purposeful—that we are badass women worthy of the same love we give to this world.

To Kristin, I am forever grateful for the way you make me feel seen, heard, and loved. Thank you for holding space in some of the darkest times.

To Kama, thank you for your wisdom and light. You see my soul and love me as I am.

To every woman who has held space, made me feel seen, heard, loved, worthy, enough, empowered—I see you, and I thank you.

To **my extended family**, it's amazing to be surrounded by so many supportive people. Coming from a large Midwestern family (on both sides) instantly provides you with a community of people who love you deeply. I want to especially thank the creators of this incredible community: Papa Ken and Nana (rest her soul), Grandma Sue and Papa Ray (my namesake).

To Aunt Aimee, thank you for showing me the importance of words and vulnerability. You are like a second mother to me, and I am so thankful for the life-giving advice you always share.

To Aunt Brenda, thank you for our conversation in Northstar in 2014. Because of you I went to the Center for Balanced Living. You saved my life.

To Aunt Jane, thank you for watching over me and keeping me safe—my guardian angel in the sky. To every person in my family, I love you all.

To the **doctors, therapists, dietitians, yoga teachers, health professionals**, and medical support who kept me going and showed me how to truly reclaim movement, my relationship with food, my body, and my life: thank you from the bottom of my heart. Specifically, thank you to Aysia, Dr. Hill, Dr. Jennifer Carter, Dr. Megan LaVoy, Dr. Ally Barry, Jennifer Kreatsoulas, Caila Yates, Jenn Kryz, Tammy Lyons, Marisa Tingle, and the Balanced Yoga teaching team. You have helped me get to where I am today. I would be lost without your guidance, expertise, and support.

To my **teachers** and fellow **writers** who showed me truly how powerful sharing our stories can be. Because of you, I'm writing and will forever see the world through pen on paper. Especially Mrs. Thomas, Ms. Klenz, and Ms. Xenos: Thank you for showing me at my lowest point that one day I will heal and share my story to empower those to come.

To my **publishing team**: thank you for seeing me, for believing in my story, and my mission.

To Ryland, thank you for giving me one of the most healing experiences of my life. The way you captured my essence through your camera lens and made me feel like an absolute goddess, you showed me there is so much beauty in loving who I am, exactly as I am.

To my first editor, Babette, thank you for holding my story with so much love and care. I did not realize the story I was writing had only just begun. Thank you for challenging me to dig deeper, to not tell people what they should learn from these pages, and instead, let my stories and words speak for themselves.

To the entire Peacock Proud Press team, especially Laura, Wendy, and Jana, thank you for empowering me to believe in the power of my story. Thank you for seeing my light and for adding so much more. I truly would not be writing this page without you all, and for that I am forever grateful.

Finally, to **every single place** I have been and seen and explored; to **every human** who has given me grace and compassion and love; to each person who shows up just as they are; to all the younger souls who need to be seen and heard; to every trail I have embarked on showing me each path I take will lead to something I could never have imagined; to the mountaintops for showing me how far I can expand; to the waters that show me each day there are highs and lows and unknown waves to be explored; to the very breath in my lungs reminding me each day I am enough just as I am—and so are you. **I am filled with deep gratitude.**

About the Author

At seventeen, Ally Rae Pesta was diagnosed with a complex eating disorder. She has been in recovery for over ten years. Raised in Cleveland, Ohio, Ally now lives in Denver, Colorado, where she works as an Eating Disorder Recovery Coach, a 200-HR Certified Yoga Teacher, and a Certified Run Coach. Ally is also a sexual assault survivor who empowers others to reclaim

freedom and power over their body in a loving, worthy, and healing way.

From personal and professional experience, Ally knows how to use joyful movement to aid and support herself and others in their recovery journey. She has swum ten miles from one end of Cleveland to the other, taught yoga in juvenile delinquent centers, run marathons, and serves as a leader of disability communities. Now, instead of endlessly monitoring calories and critiquing her body, Ally celebrates what her body is capable of. She's also passionate about teaching others to embrace the freedom to move, enjoy food, and live a large, fulfilling, and meaningful life of purpose beyond their body.

You are meant for a life of purpose beyond your body.

For additional resources, coaching,
booking an author event, or to learn more, visit
https://www.allyrae.co/

Follow Ally
Instagram @allyraepesta
TikTok @allyrae_co

Contact Ally directly by email
ally@allyrae.co

Made in the USA
Columbia, SC
10 October 2023

24253601R00155